A Return to the Spirit

A Return to the Spirit
Questions and Answers

Martin Lings

FONS VITAE
QUINTA ESSENTIA

First published in 2005 by
Fons Vitae
49 Mockingbird Valley Drive
Louisville, KY 40207
http://www.fonsvitae.com

Library of Congress Control Number: 2005927162

ISBN 1-887752-74-9

With thanks to Graeme Vanderstoel
for the photography on page 86.

This book was typeset by Neville Blakemore, Jr.

Printed in Canada.

Contents

Martin Lings, Cairo, Egypt, 2004.

One of the great privileges of my life has been to know Dr. Martin Lings, whom I first met through my Patronage of the Temenos Academy which, in turn, came about through an introduction to Dr. Kathleen Raine by Sir Laurens Van der Post. All three of these remarkable people have provided untold inspiration and support not only to myself, but to many others besides. Thus their absence from the scene makes the world a poorer place – poorer for the fact that they constantly reminded us of that invisible dimension in our existence which forms the underlying pattern of all manifestation and which has been so cruelly and brutally abused in our age.

In Dr Lings' case, he saw beneath the surface of things and helped us to penetrate the veil behind which lies the sacred meaning to so many of life's mysteries. He helped us to look beyond the literal and to comprehend that there are many layers of meaning within the hidden universe – something which science is now at last beginning to recognize through the acknowledgement of an inherent order and harmony to the world about us and within us.

I used to look forward so much to what became an annual visit from Martin Lings when I had a chance to explore with him some of his inner discoveries, whether in the world of Shakespeare or of Sufism. One of Martin Lings' greatest legacies – apart from his insights into the true significance of many of Shakespeare's plays and his remarkable biography of the Prophet Muhammad – must surely be his timely reminder to us that Sufism, of which he was such a distinguished proponent, has always been at the spiritual heart of Islam, constantly reiterating the unshakable and sacred truths of love, compassion and forgiveness which seem to lie at the very sources of the light that lightens our darkness and which, if it illuminates our hearts, can engender that peace we all seek. It is an illuminated peace which I pray is now enfolding the departed spirit of dear Martin Lings…

Martin Lings, Maadi, Cairo, Egypt.

Martin Lings

"Lives of great men all remind us
  We can make our lives sublime ..."

"To behold beauty is to become oneself beautiful."

"Beholding His glory, we ourselves are transformed
  from glory unto glory."

Faced with the daunting task of writing the Introduction to *A Return to the Spirit* and a collection of tributes to Martin Lings, I reached instinctively to my betters, and the above lines from Longfellow, Plotinus, and St. Paul came immediately to mind. One of the problems I face in writing this Introduction is to resist the impulse to latch onto hyperboles and superlatives, which Lings would have disapproved of, so I shall proceed mundanely and work up to what I want to say.

We all need role models. Infants need parents and siblings to show them how to become human- as the account of the Wolf Boy (a boy who was snatched from his parents and raised by wolves) conclusively attests; he walked on all fours and attained only their level of competences.

Moving on to a fully human plane, I remember the time when one of our grand-daughters, Sierra, was six years old. Her best friend at the time was Pillar, who was six months older and about two inches taller. I can still visualize vividly Sierra standing on tiptoe with her face only inches away from Pillar's, mouthing Pillar's words the moment they reached her ears. I could already see her assimilating Pillar's more advanced vocabulary in the way sponges soak up water. Two years later Sierra chanced to be visiting on an evening when a seminar was meeting in my living room. My wife reported that she spent a long time peeking through a crack in the door jam, completely glued to what was going on. When the students left she ran to me in the living room sobbing, "I so want to be in college, and I'm only in first grade!" It seemed as if all the sorrows of the universe were compressed into her lamenting wail.

Spiritually the principle is the same. Adults need role models as much as children do, for we too need moulds to pour our lives into. God is the ultimate model, of course, but because God is infinite and there is no commensurability between the finite and the Infinite, we need intermediates to help us bridge the gap. Hence, incarnations and prophets, of which Martin Lings has given us a beautiful example in his biography of Muhammad.

I am working up to my main point, which is that Martin Lings has been a role model for me, but let me begin at the beginning.

In his *Return to the Spirit*, Lings gives Frithjof Schoun unqualified credit for setting him on the path to the Spirit, and I can do the same. But Martin Lings played an important part in directing me to Schuon, which is the story I want to tell here.

It begins in the Fall of 1969 on the eve of my departure for a nine- month trip around the world, leading a group of students for an academic year studying the world's religions on location. Clearing my desk of the final days' mail before I left, I opened a packet containing a book titled *In the Tracks of Buddhism* by one Frithjof Schuon. I was well versed in Buddhism, but glancing at the book's Table of Contents, I noticed a chapter titled "Buddhism's Ally in Japan: Shinto or the Way of the Gods." I was not well versed in Shinto, and as I would have to lecture on that subject while in Japan, I stuffed the book into my flight bag. The timing of the book's arrival seems, in retrospect, to have been providential. Before Shinto's sacred shrine at Ise, symbolic center of the nation of Japan, under its giant cryptomeria and at low tables in the rest of the house for pilgrims, the Way of the Gods opened before me. Ise's atmosphere could itself be credited with that opening, but only if I add that it was Schuon's insights that enabled me to sense within that atmosphere—its dignity, beauty, and repose—an intellective depth. I came to see how ancestors could seem less fallen than their descendants and thereby serve, when revered, as doorways to transcendence. I saw how virgin nature—especially its grand phenomena: sun, moon, thunder, lightning, and the sky and earth that are their containers—could be venerated as the most transparent symbols of the divine. Above all, I saw how Shinto could be seen as the most intact instance we have today of an archaic hyperborean shamanism that swept in both directions from Siberia to encompass the world.

Two months later, in India, the same thing happened. Perusing a bookstore in Madras my eye fell on a study of Vedanta, *The Language of the Self*, by Frithjof Schuon. This time I didn't hesitate. For the remaining weeks I was in India I walked with that book under my arm and I was happy.

Would one believe a third installment? In Iran the leading Islamist pointed me to Schuon's *Understanding Islam* as the best book on Islam in English.

From there on events took on a truly strange and providential turn. In Sweden I was swaying while holding onto a subway strap when someone recognized me from a television program I had been on. He had just time before I got off at the next stop to hand me his calling card and ask me to phone him. When I did that, he invited my wife and me to supper, and when we entered his apartment, we found its walls covered with enlarged photographs of Native Americans. He was Joseph Epes Brown, who was earning his doctorate with Professor Hultekrans, the leading Western authority on American Indians. The noose was tightening. When I had recounted the journey that we were on and that we had just come from Iran and Hossein Nasr, he was well acquainted with the turf and knew Schuon and his followers well. Bypassing small talk I told him that I was persuaded that all authentic religions are valid revelations, but that left me with the problem of relativism. We could not make it a long evening because we had to take an early morning flight to London, the last stop on our journey. He said that the problem of relativism was not insuperable but that it would take longer to spell out, and as we had to leave he gave me the telephone number of one Martin Lings.

Lings was the Keeper of the Near Eastern manuscripts at the British Museum and invited me to visit him in his office. When I traced the remarkable sequence of events that had brought me to his door, subtly, ever so subtly- I don't remember exactly how- he suggested that there might be a kind of brotherhood (I would not have known the word *tariqa* then) that linked the people I had met on my journey and dropped the hint that I might learn about it through Seyyed Hossein. The rest of this story needs no telling here, for it is recorded in history.

I recall two other face-to-face meetings with Martin Lings. We must have been attending a conference in New Delhi, and one afternoon were all taken on an excursion to the Taj Mahal. I have an indelible visual memory of Martin squinting up at the calligraphy on the inside of the entrance gate, reading it to us as he unscrambled words from the overlapping lines of the artistic writing.

The final encounter was when I visited him in his home on the outskirts of London and was treated, before supper, to a tour of his exquisite garden. He lingered lovingly over each flowering plant, and described how it was orchestrated for its contribution to the garden's total effect. This was beauty incarnated through the works of his hands. Others, I feel sure, will comment on the perfect timing of his death. Having just put the finishing touches on his last book, *A Return to the Spirit*, he went out for a last look at his garden before his soul returned to that Spirit.

Like everyone else who knew him intimately, I revered him for being the saint he was. The book in hand cannot possibly equal the beauty of his *Sufi Saint of the Twentieth Century*, but those of us who are contributing to it will in effect be doing our best to enter a tribute to a Sufi saint of the twenty-first century.

Huston Smith
July 8, 2005

CHAPTER ONE

How Did I Come to Put First Things First?

If this question were to be worded: "To whom am I most indebted for the knowledge of how to put first things first?" the answer would be, beyond any doubt, to Frithjof Schuon. It is indeed remarkable how many of the titles of his books can be said to sum up his whole literary output. This applies even to writings that one seldom thinks of in the same line of thought, for example *Logic and Transcendence* and *Having a Center*. The word "Having" may be said to stand for everything that concerns the individual, logic included, whereas "Center" stands for everything that transcends the individual. The duality in question is more specifically dominant in other titles: *Spiritual Perspectives and Human Facts*, *The Roots of the Human Condition*, *The Transfiguration of Man*, *From the Divine to the Human*; and let us mention in passing what a blessed antidote this last title is to one of the twentieth century's slogans in praise of itself, "from the subhuman to the human." In *The Transcendent Unity of Religions* there is the same vast and compelling sweep of vision, as also in *Esoterism as Principle and as Way*. But rather than list all his books, let us sum up for ourselves: the Sole Ultimate Reality of Absolute, Infinite Perfection, and the predicament of man, made in the image of that Perfection, an image from which he has fallen and to which he must return on his way to the final reintegration into his Divine Source, here lies the essential theme of Schuon's writing.

It was not, however, the books of Schuon that first brought me into relationship with him, for the simple reason that when I stood most in need of them they did not yet exist. But in the mid-thirties, being myself then in my mid-twenties, I came upon the books of René Guénon, and I realized that in them, more than ever before, I was face to face with the truth. From my childhood I had seen that something was very wrong with the world and I was conscious of a nostalgia for past times. What struck me above all was the extreme ugliness of the modern civilization. Why had I not been born into an earlier age? As to religion, by the time I was a student at Oxford, I had altogether given up any form of worship except individual prayer. But man is essentially, by his very nature, religious, and if he ceases to follow the religion he was brought up in, he will be likely to make a creed of something else. Looking back, I see now that I made for myself a "religion" of beauty, centred on nature and on art. All this, including the nostalgia that accompanied it, was thrust into the background by Guénon's books. But at the same time it was in a sense transferred to a higher level. My new-found knowledge of esoterism caused vibrations in higher reaches of my intelligence, reaches that had previously been in a semi-dormant state for want of a truly metaphysical object; and that awakening meant that the deeper reaches of my will were impelled to vibrate with spiritual aspirations.

My intelligence had never been able to accept the exclusivist idea that there is only one valid religion. But now it had learned and most readily accepted the truth that the great religions of the world, all of them equally Heaven-sent in accordance with the various needs of different sectors of humanity, can be graphically represented by points on the circumference of a circle, each point being connected with the centre, that is, with God, by a radius. The points stand for the outward aspects of the religions, whereas each radius is the esoteric path which the religion in question offers to those who seek a direct way to God in this life, and who are capable of compliance with the demands of that way of sanctification, demands far more rigorous and exacting than those of the exoteric way of salvation. I knew immediately that my place was on one of these radii that lead from the circumference to the Centre. Which radius it was to be had yet to be decided; but I was acutely conscious that I needed a way of knowledge, and I had learned from Guénon with overwhelming clarity that before I could enter upon any esoteric path I would have to find a spiritual Master and receive from him an initiation into that way. I had also learned from Guénon the profound significance of rites: "The essential and primordial purpose of all rites" is to produce "a harmonisation of the different elements of the being" and to cause "vibrations which by their repercussions throughout the immense hierarchy of states are capable of opening up a communication with the higher states."[1]

In order to be certain of performing unquestionably orthodox rites I entered the Roman Catholic Church and began to lead as intense a spiritual life as my status of being a complete novice would allow. Apart from Mass every morning and Vespers every evening, my days were centred on the Rosary, and this brought into my life the grace of a relationship with the Blessed Virgin. At the same time my book of spiritual guidance continued very definitely to be *Man and his Becoming according to the Vedanta*, and I spent some time each day learning Sanskrit, because it seemed to me likely that the final decision I had yet to make would be for Hinduism.

It was the question of that decision that preoccupied me more than anything else. I would sometimes recite the Rosary with its one *Paternoster*, seven *Aves* and one *Gloria* again and again throughout the whole night, and at certain moments—I think it was after every seventh recitation—I would make a prayer, in the conviction that the Blessed Virgin would add her prayers to mine in response to my *ora pro nobis nunc* (pray for us now). My supplication was always one and the same, that I should find a truly great spiritual Master who would take me as his disciple, initiate me into the Way, and guide me to its End.

About this time, in the autumn of 1937, I learned that I had narrowly missed just such a Master as the man I prayed to find, a great Algerian Sufi Shaykh, who had died some three years previously; and I was told in this connection that a group of Sufis had been formed in Switzerland by a man who had been a disciple of that Master. Meantime I myself was becoming more and more conscious of my roots in Christianity. Four hundred years previously every Englishman had been a Catholic. Guénon, it was true, did not hold out much hope of finding an initiatic way in Christendom. But might not the Blessed Virgin find me just such a way? However, Hinduism still seemed the most likely possibility for me.

I increased my efforts; but the more I prayed, the more I heard about the group of Sufis in Switzerland; and one morning I woke up with the realisation that Heaven had placed within me the certitude that the leader of that group was in fact the answer to my prayer.

My first reaction was strangely tinged with a hint—no more than that—of disappointment and reluctance. Poised between Hinduism and Christianity, I was now told to go in a direction towards which I had had no leaning. Needless to say, I did not presume to set one radius of the circle above another. But whereas, apart from the two of my choice, I had felt strongly drawn towards Taoism by the relatively little that Guénon wrote of it, I had not felt any particular leanings towards Sufism. However, I had prayed, and I was sure that the Blessed Virgin had prayed, and now the prayer had been answered.

I was unable to take any action immediately, but after some weeks I made my way to Basle in Switzerland, and I knocked at the door of the house of which, in answer to tentative inquiries, I had been given the address. A man opened the door, and as I did not speak German fluently I said to him in French something like this: "I am an Englishman, a reader of Guénon, and I understand that you have here a Sufi order. I want to join you." He invited me to come in, and then immediately went to the telephone and I heard him ask someone to come to his house as soon as possible. He kindly gave me lunch, and then the man he had sent for arrived. It was Titus Burckhardt, and he took me for a long walk which marked the beginning of a great friendship.

That day was Tuesday, January 11th, 1938, and I was within two weeks of my 29th birthday. Titus Burckhardt was already

29, three months older than me. I told him the gist of what I have written here, and he said: "Our Shaykh"—he meant Frithjof Schuon—"lives in France, just across the border at Mulhouse, but he will be coming here on Friday." Meantime, the next day in fact, another member of the group, Leo Schaya, then a young man of about 20, the grandson of a rabbi, went to see the Shaykh and told him about me. He said: "Tell him, if he wants to join us, to enter Islam." So Titus Burckhardt received me into Islam. From now on, he was to be known to me as Sidi Ibrāhīm ᶜIzz ad-Dīn, "Sidi" being the North African dialectical form of Sayyidī (literally "My Lord"). He then taught me how to say the prayers, which meant that I had changed from learning Sanskrit to learning Arabic.

When Friday afternoon came, he said to me: "I am going to the station to meet the Shaykh. Would you like to come too?" And so I met the answer to my highly demanding prayer. Despite his years—he was only 30—his appearance corresponded perfectly to all that I had prayed for. But that did not increase my certitude that he was indeed the answer to my prayer, for I was already, by the grace of Heaven, as certain as I could be. Nor has that certitude ever wavered during the 66 wonderful years that I have been privileged to be his disciple. I am still acutely conscious of that privilege despite his death in 1998.

The group in Basle at that time (there was also a smaller group in Lausanne) consisted of about eleven men and five women. For their gatherings they had rented an old building on the very edge of the Rhine, to be used—so they told the landlord—as an artists' studio. There were two or three rooms, the largest of which, overlooking the water, they had made into their *zāwiyah* (literally "corner"), a name given to a hall where Sufis hold their *majālis* ("sessions", singular *majlis*). That evening I was taken there to a *majlis*, and as I sat in the circle of men, all of them in Islamic dress (they had managed to find some garments for me also), an immense happiness dawned upon me. My yearning for an impossibility, which Guénon's message had thrust into the background, suddenly reasserted itself, but this time as a reality: I was, so it seemed, about to be reborn into an earlier age which was independent of the modern world and dominated by traditional values; and I rediscovered my "religion of beauty" as a normal setting, a kind of protective shell, for the spiritual life. It had never occurred to me that the Shaykh would give me, as part of that guidance, a whole civilization. Meantime he told me that I could make use of one of the rooms belonging to the *zāwiyah*, and I lived there for the next four months. He himself came there for two nights every weekend. It was a most blessed beginning; and in the following month he initiated me into the Way.

I had been slightly puzzled that my relationship with the blessed Virgin should have had, apparently, nothing to do with the choice that Heaven had made for me. But as I said to myself, I did not pray to her; I asked her to join her prayers to mine, to pray for me to God, and it was He who decided what I should do. This logic satisfied me; but some twenty years later we asked the Shaykh to add another name to that of his Shaykh, the Shaykh al-ʿAlawī, to distinguish us from the African ʿAlawīs. We thought he would give us one of his names, but to our surprise he said: "Our *ṭarīqah* (literally "way", as a Sufi order is called) is *Maryamiyyah*, that is, of Mary; and he told us that more than once she had made it clear to him that she had chosen us for herself, and that she was our protective patroness. He went so far as to say: "It is not we who have chosen her; it is she who has chosen us." And so, after all, my *Ave Maria*, repeated such a multitude of times, had not been out of line with my final orientation. She herself would have been fully aware of this, but we, as yet, had had no knowledge of it. "Why did she choose us?" the Shaykh was asked. He answered that we did not need to know, but on another occasion, when the same question was asked, he said: "A possible answer is this: she herself is a Jewish princess of the House of David; she is also the mother of the founder of Christianity; and she stands, in Islam, at the summit of the hierarchy of women. She loves all three of these religions, and religion in general, as we do. Moreover, several of our men and women are of Jewish origin, and still more are of Christian origin, in addition to the many

6

that were born and brought up in Islam; and like her, we are much more interested in what these three religions have in common than we are in what separates them from one another. So in a sense we stand on her territory." But in fact we had not been mistaken in anticipating that he would give us his own name, because it is generally accepted, in Sufism, that every great Master, in addition to being a mysterious prolongation of the Prophet, prolongs also in a certain way one of those spiritual lights who preceded Islam.[2] And one day, when the Shaykh was asked if we could consider him to be, like his own Master, a prolongation of Jesus,[3] he said: "No, I am Maryamī ", that is, a prolongation of Mary.

In connection with the exceptional nature of the Order to which my prayers had led me, a nature responsible, as we have just seen, for its having been chosen by the great Lady after whom it is named, I feel obliged to mention yet another immensely exalted spiritual authority who, so it would seem, has indicated that he likewise has a particularly close relationship with the same Order.

In the mid-thirties, largely as a result of having read the books of Guénon, Titus Burckhardt had gone to Morocco in search of a spiritual way and had become the disciple of Mawlay ᶜAlī ad-Darqāwī in Fez, the grandson of the great Mawlay al-ᶜArabī ad-Darqāwī. It was not long before this that Frithjof Schuon had been to Mustaghanem in Algeria and had become the disciple of Shaykh Aḥmad al-ᶜAlawī who had died the following year, in 1934. That same day of his death, Sidi ᶜĪsā Nūr ad-Dīn, who several months previously had returned to Switzerland, was plunged into a remarkable state of illumination which lasted for three days and from which he knew, amongst other things, that he himself had the right, and therefore the duty, to take disciples if they presented themselves, which they did not fail to do, and to found a branch of his Master's Order in Europe. He felt prompted to write a letter to Guénon who, in his immediate reply, broke to him the news of the Shaykh's death, adding that the simultaneity of the spiritual experience was a clear sign that he, Sidi ᶜĪsā Nūr ad-Dīn, was his Shaykh's successor.

All this, and no doubt much more, was recounted by Sidi Ibrāhīm to his Moroccan Darqāwī Shaykh in Fez, and when, about a year later, Sidi Ibrāhīm had to return to his home in Basle, his Shaykh counselled him to become the disciple of Shaykh ᶜĪsā Nūr ad-Dīn. "But we will remain in touch with each other", he added.

The contents of these last two paragraphs were still fresh in men's minds when I myself arrived in Basle; and shortly after I had become the disciple of Shaykh ᶜĪsā Nūr ad-Dīn, I vividly remember Sidi Ibrāhīm coming to the *zāwiyah* where I was living and where others of the friends were often congregated, and in his hand was a letter which, as he told us, he had just received from Fez: "I must translate this remarkable letter to you. I am sure that Mawlay ᶜAlī would wish me to do so, since it has a message for us all." Then he translated the letter from Arabic into German, which I was already beginning to understand fairly well, though once or twice I had to ask him to give me the French.

The letter was based on an incident in the life of the Prophet which is recorded by most of the traditionalists. The gist is as follows: one day when the Prophet was with some of his closest Companions they heard him say, in a moment of silence, as if speaking to himself: "O my brethren!" They expected him to continue but instead, after a pause, he repeated the same words, and then again, a third time. Finally, one of the Companions ventured to say: "O Messenger of God, are not we your brethren?" He answered: "No, ye are my companions." Then, instead of quoting the exact words which follow, Mawlay ᶜAlī paraphrased the rest of the Tradition to the effect that the Prophet's brethren would be men of the last days and that they would enter his religion because they had seen "black on white", interpreted as meaning through the influence of books which they had read. Then he added, clearly with reference to Shaykh ᶜĪsā and his disciples: "Ye are among the brethren referred to by the Prophet in this Tradition."

Some twenty years later the already mentioned Leo Schaya (Sidi ᶜAbd al-Quddūs) went to Morocco and visited there, in Casablanca, one of the most revered Sufis of that time, the old and blind Shaykh Muḥammad at-Tādilī, who quoted to him the above mentioned Tradition, and made exactly the same comment that Mawlay ᶜAlī ad-Darqāwī had made.

There is also yet another sign, which is quite independent of the two signs that we have just recounted. It could be said that the Azhar University in Cairo is what might be termed the educational centre of the Islamic world, at any rate as far as concerns the main body of Muslims, and it has had that function since its foundation over a thousand years ago. In the second half of the last century one of its better students, an Egyptian named ᶜAbd al-Halīm Maḥmūd, after having taken his degree with high honours, accepted an invitation to go for a year to the Sorbonne. During that time in Paris he read some of the books of René Guénon which he considered to be of the very greatest importance.

On his return to Egypt he was given a post on the staff of the Azhar. Apart from his work there, he was himself a member of a Sufi order, whence his interest in Guénon. The years passed, and in the late sixties he was appointed Rector of the Azhar. By that time, in his private life, he was already recognized as a Sufi Shaykh and had several disciples.

In April 1969 a young couple arrived in Egypt from America, having read those of Guénon's books which were available in English at that time. It was *The Crisis of the Modern World* which, perhaps more than any other of the books, had brought them to the decision that if they wished to lead a spiritual life, which they now saw clearly to be the only life worth leading, they must escape from the West, that is, from the modern civilization, and find a spiritual Master in the East.

To come now to the point of these remarks, they succeeded in making contact with Shaykh ᶜAbd al-Halīm Maḥmūd at the Azhar, and he allowed them to visit him more than once. But finally, when they asked if he would take them as disciples, he said: "Your place is not here, but there is a branch of the order to which I belong, the Shādhilī *ṭarīqah*, which has been recently established in Switzerland on the basis of the teachings of René Guénon. It is there that you should go for spiritual guidance." They followed his advice, and it is from them that I received all the information that I have just set down about their visits to the Azhar.

As to Shaykh ᶜAbd al-Halīm, he wrote a book on the Shādhilī *ṭarīqah*, entitled *Qaḍiyyatu 't-Taṣawwuf—al-Madrasatu 'sh-Shādhiliyyah*, comprising four chapters, one of which is devoted to Guénon. It has been published in Cairo by Dār al-Maʿārif, in at least three editions. It is also of interest to note that he refers to Schuon as an overwhelmingly authoritative knower (*'ālim ḍalī'*), mentioning specifically his remarkable book, *Eye of the Heart* (see p. 297 of *Qaḍiyyatu 't-Taṣawwuf,* Cairo, 1999). Shaykh ᶜAbd al-Halīm is still remembered and revered, not only in Egypt but also in Syria and Lebanon and other parts of the Near East.

Shortly after his return from Mustaghanem Shaykh ᶜĪsā had given a lecture on Sufism in Basle and he himself was still wearing the Arab clothes he had worn in Algeria. The then eighteen years old Leo Schaya attended this lecture and was so overwhelmed by it that he went then and there to the lecturer and asked if he might be his disciple. His request was accepted.

Not long after this lecture the Shaykh decided that for anyone living in Switzerland the disadvantages of not conforming outwardly to the ways of the Swiss were greater than the advantages. But in private it was different, and at the weekly *majālis* he insisted that everyone should be impeccably dressed in traditional Islamic garments.

Those of his disciples who no longer lived with their parents were told to reserve one room in their house for prayer. It should be entirely in Islamic style, as if it was the extension of a mosque. The other rooms should also reflect our perspective, but in a more subtle way. The Shaykh himself, greatly gifted for painting, was intensely sensitive to form and colour, and he quickly devised a qualitative, harmonious, simple and restful style for the other rooms in which they would have sometimes to receive members of their family and acquaintances, most of whom were to be kept in ignorance of the *ṭarīqah*. The Shaykh was always interested in the houses of his disciples. The nearest thing to the soul is the body, then the clothes in which it is dressed, then the rooms it lives in, and to the end of his life he was continually asked for advice with regard to the choice of such things as carpets, curtains and other objects of internal decoration. As to those who still lived with their parents, they were told to reserve a corner of their bedroom for their spiritual life, and they were encouraged to visit the *zāwiyah* as much as possible, and that could be done at any hour of the day or night. Each of us had two keys, one to open the door of a house not far from the entrance to the Cathedral, Basle Minster, high up on the cliffs above the Rhine, and the second key—after going down flights and flights of stairs—to open the door of the premises of the *zāwiyah*, at the water's edge.

Other injunctions which the Shaykh then gave by word of mouth were later set down in writing, and the text in question, *Our Perspective in a Few Words*, is still regularly distributed to newcomers. It begins with a definition of spirituality: "No worldly distractions, passions, ambitions. The spiritual first. Living for the spiritual." The Shaykh was also, from the very beginning, insistent that the truly spiritual man must always be a personification of nobility. Again and again I was reminded, by what he said, that Plato had defined his ideal state as an "aristocracy", a word often used by the Shaykh, who also insisted that the inward treasure of spirituality calls for the outward virtue of dignity. In this connection he demanded of his disciples "language that is correct, not slovenly, both from the point of view of elocution as well as from that of grammar." Already before my arrival he had forbidden them ever to utter the German-Swiss dialect on the premises of the *zāwiyah*. As a result, most of his Basle disciples took to addressing each other always in pure German, and only relapsed into the hideous dialect when they had to do so for family reasons. In general we were made conscious that the Platonic dictum "Beauty is the splendour of the True" signifies that when that splendour is too

11

dim there must be a corresponding insufficiency of Truth in the intelligence.

Much has been written about the providential necessity of Schuon's writings as a sequel to those of Coomaraswamy and Guénon, so I will limit myself to pointing out three main aspects of that need. Firstly it was important that the work of these great pioneers, and that of Guénon in particular, should have a living prolongation of younger writers who would keep it in the foreground of the minds of serious readers by continual quotations and references and developments. By far the most outstanding of these heirs and perpetuators is Frithjof Schuon. Titus Burckhardt must also be mentioned in this context.

Secondly, the work of a pioneer is almost bound to be fraught with simplifications and generalizations, and Schuon, who never simplifies and who, on the contrary, continually makes us aware of the extreme complexity of things, was providentially just the follower-on that was needed to fill in the inevitable gaps, to tie up loose threads left hanging, and, by admitting and explaining unmentioned exceptions, to justify valid generalizations.

Thirdly, and most importantly, there was a certain order of development that had to be followed. We could say in general that the main theme of both Guénon and Schuon is esoterism. On this basis, the major part of Guénon's writing could be summed up as "esoterism as principle with a view to the way." But it remained for Schuon to write *Esoterism as Principle and as Way*, the title of which does justice to his qualification to write about what follows initiation as well as about what precedes it. In this respect the writings of the elder man can be seen as a preparation for those of his successor. It is true that Guénon could be said to have bridged the gap with *Man and his Becoming*, but only to a certain extent. Unlike Schuon, it was never his function to be a spiritual Master.

Before closing this tribute to the greatest writer of our times, as I believe him to be, I would like to let him speak a little for himself.

It goes without saying that the ideas of the 'Great Spirit' and of the primary importance of the invisible as compared with the visible are natural to man. Now what is natural to human consciousness proves by that very fact its essential truth, for the whole point of human intelligence is that it should be altogether up to grasping reality. We have heard someone say that the wings of a bird prove the existence of air, and that in the same way the religious phenomenon, common *a priori* to all peoples, proves the existence of its contents, namely God and the after-life, which is to the point if one takes the trouble to examine the argument in depth.[4]

As regards the Renaissance, man's change from being symbolist to being rationalist, Schuon says:

This transition from objectivism to subjectivism reflects and repeats in its own way the fall of Adam and the loss of Paradise; in losing a symbolist and contemplative perspective, founded both on impersonal intelligence and on the metaphysical transparency of things, man has gained the fallacious riches of the *ego*; the world of divine images has become a world of words. In all cases of this kind, heaven— or a heaven—is shut off from above us without our noticing the fact, and we discover in compensation an earth long unappreciated, or so it seems to us, a homeland which opens its arms to welcome its children and wants to make us forget all lost Paradises; it is the embrace of *Māyā*,[5] the sirens' song; *Māyā*, instead of guiding us, imprisons us. The Renaissance thought that it had discovered man, whose pathetic convulsions it admired; from the point of view of laicism in all its forms, man as such had become, to all intents and purposes, good, and the earth too had become good and looked immensely rich and unexplored; instead of living only "by halves" one could at last live fully, be fully man and fully on earth; one was no longer a kind of half-angel, fallen and exiled; one had become a whole being, but by the downward path.[6]

13

Of one of the consequences of this fall and of the worldly expansion which resulted from it, namely the tragic crushing of
the Red Indians of North America, he writes elsewhere:

> This great drama might be defined as the struggle, not only
> between a materialistic civilization and another that was
> chivalrous and spiritual, but also between urban civiliza-
> tion (in the strictly human and evil sense of this term, with
> all its implications of 'artifice' and 'servility') and the king-
> dom of Nature considered as the majestic, pure, unlimited
> apparel of the Divine Spirit. And it is from this idea of the
> final victory of Nature (final because it is primordial) that
> the Indians draw their inexhaustible patience in the face of
> the misfortunes of their race; Nature, of which they feel
> themselves to be embodiments, and which is at the same
> time their sanctuary, will end by conquering this artificial
> and sacrilegious world, for it is the Garment, the Breath,
> the very Hand of the Great Spirit.[7]

Let us now revert to *From the Divine to the Human*, this time to
the chapter on "The Message of the Human Body":

> The gait of the human being is as evocative as his vertical
> posture; whereas the animal is horizontal and only advances
> towards itself—that is, it is enclosed within its own form—
> man, in advancing, transcends himself; even his forward
> movement seems vertical, it denotes a pilgrimage towards
> his Archetype, towards the celestial Kingdom, towards God.
> The beauty of the front of the human body indicates the
> nobleness, on the one hand of man's vocational end, and on
> the other of his manner of approaching it; it indicates that
> man directs himself towards God and that he does so in a man-
> ner that is 'humanly divine', if one may say so. But the back
> of the body also has its meaning: it indicates, on the one hand
> the noble innocence of the origin, and on the other hand the
> noble manner of leaving behind himself what has been tran-
> scended; it expresses, positively, whence we have come and,

negatively, how we turn our backs to what is no longer our-selves. Man comes from God and he goes towards God; but at the same time, he draws away from an imperfection which is no longer his own and draws nearer to a perfection which is not yet his. His 'becoming' bears the imprint of a 'being'; he is that which he becomes, and he becomes that which he is.[8]

The following quotation serves as an example of Schuon's masterly rebuttals of increasingly prevalent errors which the official representatives of religion seem to be incapable of cor-recting.

We have heard it said that the boundless happiness of Para-dise is impossible since it would end in boredom for lack of contrast; it seems that in order to appreciate happiness there must be points of comparison and reference, and thus suf-fering. This view is erroneous for several reasons.

He begins his refutation by pointing out that the opinion in ques-tion is false even as regards this world, let alone the hereafter:

In the first place, a man who is morally and intellectually unimpaired satisfies the need for contrasts or change by his discernment, detachment and discipline; in the second place, a superior man has the intuition of archetypes or essences and is kept in a state of supernatural equilibrium by the fact that his vision opens out onto the Infinite. In Paradise, noth-ing can fade, either objectively or subjectively, since things and perceptions are ceaselessly renewed through their con-tact with the Divine Infinitude; man thus finds himself freed, doubtless not from a certain need for compensating activi-ties or rhythms, but from the psychological or moral neces-sity of contrasting changes. The metaphysical proof of this is the Divine Felicity itself, which does not suffer in the least from being without shadows, but which necessarily contains 'dimensions' to the extent that our way of envis-aging the Divine Order is linked to this realm.[9]

Finally let us end our quotations with a passage of immense practical importance in which the author seems to be speaking directly and as it were separately to each one of his readers, for all by way of warning and for some by way of invitation.

> Knowledge saves only on condition that it enlists all that we are, only when it is a way which tills and which transforms and which wounds our nature as the plough wounds the earth...Metaphysical knowledge is sacred. It is the right of sacred things to demand of man all that he is.[10]

We have here an insistence upon the need for total commitment which is a dominant note throughout Schuon's writings; and as a guide of souls he was especially generous in his bestowal of the means by which that commitment can be achieved, knowing, as he well did, the great difficulty, especially for anyone born, brought up and educated in the modern Western world, of drawing together all the scattered psychic elements into a perfection of single-minded sincerity.[11]

The Shaykh as he was when I first met him.

Frithjof Schuon, Venice, Italy.

Shaykh ʾIsa and Sidi Abū Bakr, Basle, Switzerland.

CHAPTER TWO

Do the Religions Contradict
One Another?

The answer to this question is emphatically no, inasmuch as every religion is a manifestation of the One Supreme Reality. It needs nonetheless to be answered in some detail, since most of us have heard it said more than once over the years: "How is it possible to believe in religion since the different religions contradict each other?" The motive behind such remarks can never be profound, but it may vary between a would-be self-justification for not practicing religion and the desire to be thought intelligent or up to date. As to other motives given such as the mistaken supposition that the Darwinian theory of evolution has been scientifically proved to be true, whereas it has in fact no scientific basis at all, I have written about this at some length already elsewhere,[1] so I will not repeat myself here.

I am bound however to repeat in our present context what I have already said more than once elsewhere about the complete dependence of every religion upon the Divine Word, which may manifest Itself either as Book or Man. In Christianity the Word is Christ, and the New Testament is not Revelation but an inspired sacred history of the life and teaching of the Word made Flesh, whereas Judaism and Islam are based on the Word made Book. The basis of Judaism is the Pentateuch, the first five books of the Old Testament which were revealed to Moses, together with the Psalms which were revealed to David, and the basis of Islam is the Qur'ān which was revealed to Muḥammad. In the ancient religions, of which Hinduism appears to be the sole fully surviving example, there was room for both these Divine Manifestations: the Vedas are the Word made Book, and the Avatāras of Vishnu are the Word made Flesh.

It must however be clearly understood that in the religions which are based on the Word made Book, the Messenger to whom the Book is revealed is thereby to be ranked at the highest degree of sanctity, which means that some of his utterances are bound to proceed from the level of the Divine Word, even if the structure of the religion does not allow him to be worshipped. It is therefore possible for every Divine Messenger to make a statement which amounts to the same as the words of Christ, "None cometh to the Father but through me"; and there is in Islam a saying attributed to the Prophet Muḥammad to the effect that there can be no meeting with God which is not preceded by a meeting with himself. Moreover St. Thomas Aquinas says that the fact of a Divine Person having manifested Itself in one human nature does not prevent It from doing so in another human nature.[2] We are thus enabled to speak symbolically of the Word as a precious stone of many facets. It is true that the above quoted words of Christ are altogether central to Christianity, whereas the equivalent saying of Muḥammad cannot be said to have the same place in Islam. We did not however quote them to distinguish this from that, but on the contrary to identify each with the other. Both are expressions of the truth that there is no way to God except through His Word. There is therefore no question here of contradiction between two religions.

We will briefly mention here another point which might seem to some of our readers to be contradictory. The Buddha is not mentioned in the Qur'ān at all, but the Qur'ān states that for every people God has sent a messenger (X, 47), and that some of these have been mentioned whereas others have not (XL, 78; IV, 164); and since the Buddha established a religion over two thousand years ago which to this day remains in possession of a large part of the East, he must have been a messenger in the full sense of the Arabic word *rasūl*. Can it not then be said that the absence in Buddhist doctrine of any word which can reasonably be translated by the word "God" constitutes a kind of inter-religious contradiction? The answer is that Buddhism's insistence on the One Absolute Infinite Eternal Reality brings it into agreement with all other religions.

Let us now pass on to an apparent contradiction which cannot be dismissed so easily. If the religion of Islam depended on the beliefs of the average Muslim, then there would indeed be a contradiction; but Islam depends on the Qur'ān, not on human opinion that is based on Quranic verses taken out of their context.

It is a fact that most Muslims believe that Christ was not crucified, whereas Christians consider the Crucifixion to be as it were the foundation stone of their religion. Many aspects of their religion have been questioned and rejected by certain Christians: already in very early Christianity a number of differing schools of thought were hurling anathema at each other;[3] but I have never heard of any Christian that denies the Crucifixion and rejects the sign of the Cross. The Muslim denial of the Crucifixion is based on a Quranic statement isolated from its setting, combined perhaps with a natural readiness to accept what appears to be good news. The idea that God would allow one of His Messengers to be crucified is hard to accept, nor is the Christian doctrine of the Redemption easy to understand. I have heard it said: "Are we not all included in God's redemption of Adam?"

As to the whole of the Quranic passage in question (II, 37-8), having been blamed for their calumny of Mary and their denial of the Virgin birth of Christ, the Jews are then blamed for having said: *Verily we have slain the Messiah Jesus the Son of Mary, the Messenger of God* (IV, 156-7). The Qur'ān then adds the words: *And they did not slay him and they did not crucify him, but it seemed to them that they had done so.*

Now we must bear in mind that when the Prophet Muḥammad was once asked: "When did you become a Prophet", he answered: "I was a Prophet when Adam was between water and clay." In other words, Prophethood is not of this world, but transcends time and space. As we have seen, every Messenger has two natures, one which is transcendent

22

and one which is human. There is never any question in Christianity of the Divine Nature of Christ having been crucified. As for the Jews, they looked on him as a man who falsely claimed to be the Messiah. But instead of saying "we have slain this usurper", they said, with typical Jewish sarcasm: "We have slain the Messiah." The Qur'ān denies this possibility, and then adds what are, in our context, the all important words: *But it seemed to them that they had done so.* Why did it seem to them that they had done so? Precisely because they had seen the dead body of Christ's human nature before them on the Cross. There is therefore no mutual contradiction here between Christianity and Islam.

In this context it should perhaps be mentioned that exoterism, as opposed to esoterism, is a domain in which there are bound to be apparent contradictions—apparent but not real, because exoterism is no more than the result of a gradual falling away from an esoterism which alone can be considered as the full reality of the religion in question. I once, not recently, attended an inter-religious congress in Delhi, and the speaker who had been invited to represent Christianity was insistent that since the Crucifixion, the only valid religion was Christianity with its Trinity of Father, Son and Holy Ghost who are, taken all together, One God. Moreover he seemed pleased to have the opportunity of being able to preach what he believed to be the one and only truth to such a diversity of non-Christians; but unknown to himself, he could hardly have chosen a less receptive setting than this for his particular theme.

The congress, being where it was, had in the nature of things been organised by Hindu Brahmins who considerably outnumbered the single representatives of the other religions. They were all of the Advaita Vedantist school and knew well that the age-old doctrine of Hinduism affirms a Divine Trinity which corresponds to the Christian Trinity but which is still in the domain of *Māyā* (illusion), being transcended by *Ātmā*, the Self, which is the One-and-Only Reality. Moreover these Hindus were particularly insistent upon the transcendence in question.

23

When the talk had come to an end, during the brief period in which others are allowed to speak, I felt obliged to point out that more than one of the Christian Saints had insisted, with no little vehemence, that beyond the Trinity there is the Supreme Reality of Absolute Infinite Eternal Perfection. Among the best known of these, to name only two, are Meister Eckhart and Angelus Silesius; and if others, no less great, remained silent on this point, it was no doubt through consideration for the vast majority of their fellow Christians for whom two different levels of Divinity, one above the other, would inevitably amount to two Gods. In mentioning this danger, Frithjof Schuon also reminds us that the main purpose of religion is to save souls rather than to convey metaphysical truths. Needless to say, he is not denying that the truth has its rights, but simply remarking that in the present state of the world certain errors have to be accepted by official representatives of religion as half-truths for fear of causing even greater errors. But in his own writings, which are addressed to metaphysicians and to those who are capable of accepting metaphysical truths as Divine Mysteries even if they cannot yet clearly understand them, he is so insistent on mentioning the truth in question that he goes so far as to speak of "the Relative Absolute"—which is, as he fully admits, something of a contradiction in terms—in order to distinguish the less higher aspect of Divinity (academically sometimes known as the Personal God) from the Supreme Summit which transcends it.

The Brahmins showed such interest in what I had said that I took the opportunity of informing these representatives of the oldest living esoterism that the final esoterism of this cycle of time, namely Sufism, the esoterism of Islam which I had been invited to represent, is in entire agreement with Hinduism in reserving a place, at the summit of the hierarchy, for Absolute Infinite Oneness which excludes all question of duality.

In Islam it is often said that God has a hundred Names, but this saying is not to be taken too literally because more than one list has been handed down to us by tradition. These Names are not all at the same level, and the chief criterion as to the level of any particular Name is whether or not it implies any plurality. The Names Lord (*ar-Rabb*) and King (*al-Malik*) suggest respectively the existence of slaves and subjects. But the highest Names, those of the Divine Essence, such as *al-Ḥaqq* the Truth (in its widest sense of Absolute Reality), *al-Qayyūm* the Absolutely Independent, *al-Aḥad* the One-and-Only, and *aṣ-Ṣamad* the Self-Sufficient, are beyond any such implication.

It is also possible for a Divine Name which usually expresses plurality to be used at the level of the Essence. It could be said that in the opening words of the Holy Tradition "I was a Hidden Treasure and I loved to be known", the Divine Name *ash-Shākir*, the Grateful, is implicitly present in its supreme sense as a Name of the Essence expressing the Gratitude of Absolute Infinite Perfection to Itself for being what It is.

Certain Names of the Essence are less obviously so, and as such they are highly informative, as for example *al-Ḥayy* the Living, which tells us that such life as we have on earth is not ours but a brief loan from the Living Himself, immensely reduced to the level of our transitory earthly existence. If the question be asked: "What is life?", a good answer, which is in fact sometimes given, is that Life is a Divine spark within us. Analogously the certitude that each one of us has of being "myself", of being "I", is just such a loan from *Anā* (the Arabic word *anā* denotes the first personal pronoun). In the Qur'ān God not only says "No god but God" and "no god but He" but also "no god but I." This brings us back to the Sanskrit word *Ātmā*, the One and Only Self of Hindu doctrine.

To revert to our chapter heading, it will, I think, have been clearly understood that difference by no means necessarily coincides with contradiction. Muslims are forbidden to drink wine, for example, though they are promised it for the higher Paradises of the Hereafter. The Eucharist, on the other hand, which consists of bread and wine, may be considered as the basic rite of Christianity, and there is a chapter in the Qur'ān of which the title, "The Table", signifies the farewell supper at which Christ established the rite of the Eucharist. The Qur'ān affirms the Christian doctrine of the transubstantiation of what the Christian Apostles ate and drank at the table by stating that the whole meal was sent down from Heaven as a sign which would be perpetual for all Christians throughout the centuries (V, 112-5).

Al-Muhaymin, the Protector, the Watcher-over, is one of the Names of God, and this Name is used in the Qur'ān of the Qur'ān itself in relation to what preceded it (V, 48). The above mentioned Quranic passage about the Eucharist is an example of that protection. It may be said to reaffirm the essence of Christianity in the face of doubts which certain heretical sects and many individuals who claim to be Christians have cast upon the idea of transubstantiation.

Conversely it should be made known to both Christians and Muslims of today that at the time of the Last Supper, and possibly even at the Supper itself, Christ predicted the revelation of the Qur'ān. It was moreover inevitable that he should do so. Without making any quotation, Frithjof Schuon has remarked in general: "It is inconceivable that Christ, when speaking of the future, should not have mentioned the one Divine Manifestation which was to take place between his two comings."

The passage in question which undoubtedly refers to the Revelation of the Qur'ān to Muḥammad is as follows: "I have yet many things to say unto you, but ye cannot bear them now. Howbeit when he, the Spirit of Truth, is come, he will guide you unto all truth: for he shall not speak of himself, but whatsoever he shall hear, that shall he speak; and he will show you the things to come."[4]

It is however an undeniable fact that not all prophesies are made primarily for the sake of those who first hear them and record them. Not without importance in this context are the words "But ye cannot bear them now." In any case Christ would have known that the majority of those who surrounded him thought that his second coming would be soon and that what he said about the Spirit of Truth was therefore bound to be identified with something far more immediate than the coming of Muḥammad some six hundred years later. It was in fact identified with the miracle of Pentecost. The descent of the tongues of flame might be said in a certain sense to indicate a coming of the Spirit of Truth, but it does not fully correspond to the words, "He shall not speak of himself, but whatsoever he shall hear, that shall he speak" which clearly refer to the Prophet's foundation of the religion of Islam, not on his own initiative of personal ideas, but on the verses of the Qur'ān which he heard revealed to him, passage by passage, throughout the rest of his life. Moreover towards the end of the preceding chapter of St. John which contains the first mention of the Spirit of Truth, the words "he will tell you all things"[5] correspond perfectly to the Quranic verses. Unlike the New Testament which providentially fulfils the Christian need for an inspired record of the life and teachings of the Word-made-Flesh, the Qur'ān does in fact "guide us into all truth" by telling us much that we did not know about the lives of Messengers and Prophets whom God has sent into the world, about the different religions and their foundation, about human nature, and above all about the Nature of God in Whose image man's nature was made.

It is not illegitimate to suppose that Christ would have known also that the full meaning of his words as recorded by St. John was not destined to be understood until over a thousand years had passed since the actual coming of the Spirit of Truth. Otherwise expressed, he would have known that the identification of his words with the miracle of Pentecost was destined to be more or less exclusively accepted by Christians until the present day.

We have more than once quoted Schuon's timely remark that "if human societies degenerate on the one hand with the passage of time they accumulate on the other hand experience in virtue of old age, however intermingled with error their experience may be."[6] It is true that the world was already in extreme old age two thousand years ago, but that old age lay hidden under the youth of Christianity and then, subsequently, also under the youth of Islam. Nonetheless, its unseen presence below the surface has now precipitated those two latest religions towards itself, that is, in the direction of old age. I myself, having briefly summed up what has just been said, have even ventured to say in more than one recent lecture given in

London, "Everyone in this room, including those who are young in years, is old, and as such we have a choice between two attributes offered us by old age, namely senility and wisdom. Despite the fact that the vast majority of our contemporaries have chosen the former of these—whence the present state of the world—it is nonetheless possible and even inevitable that some will choose wisdom, a wisdom that is calm and objective, free from the passionate prejudices which have previously been too dominant in human souls with regard to religions other than their own, a wisdom which cannot fail to rejoice in the certitude of this prediction by Christ of the coming of the Prophet of Islam. Nor can we fail to rejoice in the honour that it is directly to us, men and women of the eleventh hour, that Christ is addressing this message more than to any others."

We will close this chapter with words from the Qur'ān which in a sense sum up all that we have been saying, words which might be called the Islamic equivalent of the Christian *Credo*, compared with which they have a striking simplicity. On the one hand they are more authoritative than the *Credo* because the Qur'ān, unlike the Christian *Book of Common Prayer*, is direct Revelation from God. But on the other hand, unlike the *Credo*, they have no distinct place in the liturgy of Islam, and the average Muslim is ignorant of their existence. They give us nonetheless a definite statement, on the authority of the Word-made-Book, of the faith of the Prophet and of those who may be considered as the most spiritual of his Companions. *They believe, all of them, in God and His Angels and His Books and His Messengers. And they say: "We make no distinction between any of His Messengers"* (II, 285).

Let us add, by way of commentary on the final sentence, two utterances of the Prophet, evoked on different occasions by disregard of the principle in question: "Say not that I am better than Moses" and "Say not that I am better than Jonah."

CHAPTER THREE

Why "With All Thy Mind?"

It could be said that one of the criteria of orthodoxy in a religion is that it should provide adequate means for the fulfilment
of the following commandment in all its aspects: "Thou shalt
love the Lord thy God with all thy heart, and with all thy soul,
and with all thy mind, and with all thy strength."[1]

The most essential part of the commandment is clearly its
opening. The heart is the organ of faith, whose higher possibilities are certainty, intellection, gnosis. It is called "heart"
because it is as central and vital to the soul as the physical heart
is to the body. The function of a centre is always that of attraction and radiation, on the one hand to draw towards it the outly-
ing parts and to keep them knitted together as an integral whole,
and on the other to transmit to them, according to the measure
and the mode of their varying capacities, what it receives from
worlds which lie above and beyond it. To "love with all thy
heart" means total love. Mind and soul, which depend ulti-
mately on the heart for love of God, needed separate mention
in the commandment only because their domination by the centre was reduced at the Fall to being no more than a virtuality,
and because on the path of return to the primordial state of
loving "with all thy heart", mind-love and soul-love have a function of cause—or so it seems—in the process of re-awakening
heart-love, though they could never be fully realized except as
a result of that re-awakening. The give and take in question
correspond to the interaction of human initiative and Divine
Grace. However much the manner of expression may vary,
religions are in agreement that a minimum of effort from mind
or soul in the direction of the heart, that is, the Transcendent, is

guaranteed to call down upon itself a vivifying and growth-promoting force out of all proportion to the gesture that released it. But that human gesture needs to be continually repeated.

Loss of direct contact with the heart meant loss of that inward attraction which alone could counterbalance the centrifugal tendencies of the lower faculties. Left to their own resources, they were bound to move further and further from the centre and therefore from each other. This process of disintegration, although checked and even partially reversed for brief periods by repeated Divine interventions throughout the course of time, is inevitably now near to reaching its extremities, inasmuch as all traditions agree that we are approaching the end of this temporal cycle; and one of the most striking features of the general disintegration characteristic of modern man is an unparalleled mental independence by reason of which many minds are feverishly active and almost "acrobatically" nimble. The same lack of anchorage makes also for an abnormally hurried superficiality of judgements and conclusions.

It is this mental independence which makes so timely and so necessary the chapter on "Understanding and Believing" in Frithjof Schuon's *Logic and Transcendence*.[2] The author focuses our attention on the monstrous yet now not uncommon phenomenon of understanding metaphysical truths in the mind without any assent of belief from the soul, let alone the heart. The only remedy is re-integration, since only if the different faculties are knit closer together can the soul be brought within near enough reach of the mind to respond to the light of the doctrine, which is addressed to the mind directly. But mental understanding followed by re-integration are as a second and third stage in the path of return. In the present context we are concerned with the preliminary stage of removing obstacles. Even in the innermost aspects of religion there can be affirmations which are unattractive to the mind. But at the esoteric level all that is needed to transform that unattractiveness to its opposite is a fuller explanation. By way of example, the supreme aim and end of religion, which in Christianity is some-

times termed Deification, is perhaps in general more often referred to as the Supreme Identity; and at the beginning of the
path, after a certain very relative progress has been made, there
is a danger that the novice in question, greatly overrating that
progress, may fall into the trap (which is precisely what the
enemy of mankind wants above all) of deifying his own ego
rather than God. For this reason we find, in Sufism for example, the not infrequent insistence on referring to the Divine
Self by the third personal pronoun rather than the first. It has
more than once been said that the most perfect formulation of
the Supreme Truth is "He is He." But other Sufis have seen
that each of the three personal pronouns has its limitations. The
Shaykh al-ᶜAlawī, while admitting the inadequacy of "I" and
"Thou", points out that the third of the three has also a dis-
qualifying limitation that makes it incapable of expressing the
Absolute Reality, and this is its lack of inclusiveness.[3] To go
back to our starting point, the mind, far from being totally
enamoured of "He is He" feels as it were "left out in the cold."
But one of the greatest of the early Sufis, Abu Saᶜīd al-Kharrāz,
gives us implicitly a most satisfying solution in his answer to
the question "Through what sign knowest thou God?" He said:
"Through His Union of Opposites",[4] after which he added the
following quotation from the Qur'ān: *He is the First and the
Last, and the Outward and the Inward* (LVII, 3).

If we consider the latter of these two pairs, the Outward
and the Inward, in one of its aspects, namely Objectivity and
Subjectivity, we see that on the plane of Supreme Reality, He
(Objectivity) and I (Subjectivity) are inseparably One, while
remaining nonetheless absolutely objective and subjective; and
an aspect of that inseparability is Thou, the Archetype of the
second personal pronoun, for nothing positive exists in manifestation which is not already present in its Divine Source. It is
through Thou that I and He converse with each other, and that
communion is an aspect of the Divine Self-Sufficiency expressed by the Name *as-Ṣamad*.

As to the outer aspects of religion, the rights of intelligence
have by no means always been upheld by the authorities in ques-

tion. The mental faculties need to be appeased and re-assured; and to this end religion has no option but to sacrifice certain half-truths, not to speak of mere suppositions and conjectures, which in the past were considered as powerful motives for loving God "with all thy soul and with all thy strength."

A religion's claim to unique efficacy must be allowed the status of half-truth because there is, in fact, in the vast majority of cases, no alternative choice.[5]/ In the past it would have been as pointless for a religion to dwell on the validity and efficacy of other religions as it would be for an announcement to be made from an all-capacious lifeboat to those struggling in the waters about it that five miles away there was an equally good lifeboat./The lack of any such acknowledgement did not cause minds to falter in their worship, because each traditional civilization lived for the most part in high-walled isolation from other sectors of humanity./ Moreover, there is nothing questionable in the general notion that certain religions are defunct and have been superseded by Divine intervention. Nor can it be doubted that pseudo-religion is a possibility, since the scriptures themselves speak of false prophets. A mediaeval Christian, for example, was therefore not mentally compromised because he classed Judaism as a superseded religion or because he classed Islam as a pseudo-religion. Everyone has a right to be ignorant or mistaken about what takes place in worlds other than his own. /

But in the present age the isolating walls have for the most part been broken down. Otherwise expressed, the lifeboats are mostly within reach of each another, and lifelines even cross; and minds are inevitably troubled by thoughts which would never have assailed them in the past. In a word, it becomes difficult to dedicate the mind to the worship of God when religious authorities make claims which the intelligence sees to be in direct contradiction with what religion teaches about the nature of God.

It may be objected that if the present situation is new, globally speaking, it none the less existed in the past, if only for relatively small minorities who lived at the frontiers which sepa-

rated one theocratic civilization from another. For the last thir-
teen hundred years and more, Christians and Muslims have lived
side by side in the Near East, with ample opportunities for seeing that "the other religion" is, in fact, just as genuine as their
own. But until recent times the vast majority, including intel-
lectuals, were none the less able, in all peace of mind, to live
out their lives in the conviction that their religion alone was
truly valid. Why should not the same exclusivism still be com-
patible with mental serenity?

The answer is partly that the frontiers which separate one
perspective from another are not merely geographical. In a
theocratic civilization, men are perpetually surrounded by reminders of God and the Beyond; and this produces an "inwardness" which is both individual and collective, and which is itself a kind of isolating wall.[6] The destruction of such walls is
an evil; but the virtues they helped to maintain are indispens-
able and must be supported by other means. We have already
quoted in the last chapter[7] what Frithjof Schuon says about the
positive aspect of old age with regard to a certain collective
wisdom which human societies accumulate through experience,
despite the errors that result from degeneration. But we did not
mention his remark that the representatives of religion should
take advantage of all that is positive in being experienced and
should change their way of presenting religion by using arguments of a higher order, intellectual rather than sentimental.

/Mental dilemma is a more or less inevitable consequence
of seeking to maintain, in the modern world, all the details of
the average religious perspective which characterized one's
pious ancestors./ A striking example of this is to be seen in an
article on Jesus which a Jewish Rabbi was invited to write in
one of our leading newspapers, the purpose of the invitation
being to have an opinion which was representative of Jewry as
a whole. The Rabbi's exposition is based on the question: What
prompted Jesus to claim that he was the Messiah? A Jew, he
maintains, is well qualified to answer this question in virtue of
his special knowledge of the history of his own people, from
which he knows that expectations of the Messiah had never

been so strong as they were at that particular time. There was a kind of collective wishful thinking in the air which made it almost inevitable that someone would persuade himself and others that he was, in fact, the Lord's Anointed. The Rabbi goes on to speak appreciatively of Jesus as a man, acknowledges his excellent human qualities, emphasizes his good intentions, and excuses him for his Messianic claims.

As a purely psychological explanation of how the Christian religion came into existence, this article opens up the way for someone else to demolish Judaism by exactly the same type of argument. Another point to be noticed is that the author, so it seems, does not dare to think beyond early first century Palestine either in time or in space. He speaks almost as if the crucifixion had only just been perpetrated, closing forever, as it must have seemed to not a few, one of many chapters in the chronicle of false Messianic claims. But what of world history in the last two thousand years? What of the fact that this "false Messiah" has taken possession, spiritually speaking, of three continents and half possession of a fourth, while making considerable inroads into the fifth? And what of the God who has allowed this wide-spread, long-lasting, deep-rooted deception to take place?

In other words, a would-be demonstration of the falsity of another religion proves to be a boomerang which comes back to strike at the very heart of one's own religion. For God is the heart of every religion; and a god who would allow deception on such a colossal scale would not be worth worshipping, even by the "chosen people" whom he had protected against that deception.

On such a basis, belief can only be kept up by not following certain trains of thought which demand to be followed, and by refusing to draw certain obvious conclusions—in fact by no longer being equipped "with all thy mind", let alone loving God. Such belief is exceedingly precarious; and even if the believer in question can live out his own life in orthodoxy to the end, he has little means of fortifying others, and he is in perpetual danger of finding any day that his sons and his daughters have lapsed into agnosticism or atheism. The anti-spiritual pressures of the modern world being what they are—and this applies especially to modern education—the scales are heavily weighted against finding the only true solution, namely a more universal spiritual perspective, which means moving nearer to the Spirit and therefore "upstream" and "against the current." / On the other hand, the false solution of agnosticism is simply the next easy step down from misgivings about religion that are based on rationalism and pseudo-logic.

It seems to the Jew that to admit the Messianic claims of Jesus would amount to admitting that Judaism has been super-seded—and Christians are waiting at the door to tell him that this is indeed the case. He wrongly imagines himself to be faced, practically speaking, with a choice between Judaism and Christianity. But it would be possible—and this is certainly a solution which some orthodox Jews have individually[8] found for themselves—at least to reserve judgement about Jesus, or even to accept in his first coming a foretaste of the final and all-fulfilling Messianic advent, while continuing to cling to the God-given certainties of the Pentateuch and the Psalms. For Jews who were not swept into Christianity on the crest of its initial wave, the fact that the Messianic mission has not yet been altogether fulfilled can be taken as a sign that Judaism has not yet been superseded and as a justification for remaining faithful to the religion of Moses.

/It is relatively easy for the Jew to go half way towards the perspective of *religio perennis* simply by reserving judgement about other religions. Since Judaism is not a world religion, he can, with a clear conscience, leave other sectors of humanity to Providence in the certainty that It will take care of them. /The Christian on the other hand feels himself to be the chosen in-strument of Providence in this respect, as indeed he is, but within limits. The Church's refusal to see these limits results in a perspective which, in the modern world, runs dangerously close to the precipice of disbelief.

It is now some years since the already mentioned book *The Call of the Minaret* was published, and there is reason to think that the views of its author have moved since that time in a more universal direction. It is none the less a faithful mirror of the dilemma which faces many Christians, in particular clergymen and more especially missionaries, who come into close contact with Islam, and who cannot help being deeply impressed by its strength and its fullness as a religion. It is impossible for them to persist in calling Muḥammad a "false prophet." On the other hand they will not, or as the case may be, dare not, give up their claim that the Passion of Jesus is the sole means of man's redemption. The point of the book's title is that the muezzin's call should be for Christians as a summons to duty, "the duty of restoring to Muslims the Christ that they have missed." The author adds: "The Christ Jesus of the historic faith is an inescapable figure. It is He we must present to the world of Islam…yet how we are to do this remains a problem and a burden!" These last words are an understatement. It is almost impossible to make adult Muslims accept the Christian doctrine of Redemption, for they already have a full doctrine of Divine Grace and Mercy in another form, and the historic Jesus plays no part in it, although he remains a most benevolent and glorious onlooker. The Qur'ān calls him the Word of God and a Spirit from God; and Muḥammad testified to his second coming. In the days of the Caliphate, one of the traditional ways of wishing long life to a Caliph was to say to him: My you live long enough to give your government into the hands of Jesus, the son of Mary—Peace be on them both! But it would be impossible to introduce Jesus into the inner structure of Islam, for the building is already complete and perfect. Providence has not been waiting nearly fourteen hundred years for some Christian missionary to lay the foundation stone.

The author in question seems to have certain suspicions along these lines, and sparks of exasperation—or something akin to that—fly out from time to time: "Islam has proved in history the supreme displacer of the faith of Christ", and "The rise of Islam will always be a painful puzzle to the Christian mind." But although he speaks of "transcending difficulties", there is nothing really transcendent in the book from beginning to end, and that is its weakness. On such a basis, there can clearly be no question of "loving with all thy mind."

The same criticisms cannot be made of *A New Threshold* [9] by the Bishop of Guildford, because there is at least one remarkable outlet onto universality in a timely quotation from St. Justin Martyr's *Apology*, where the uniqueness of Christ as Redeemer is expounded at the level of the Logos and not allowed to trespass upon lower domains which are subject to multiplicity. From this point of view, the act of Redemption belongs to the Divine Nature of Jesus, not to his human nature, and since it thus transcends time and space, it cannot be limited to any historical event. "We have been taught that Christ is the First-begotten of God, and have testified that He is the Intellect (*logos*) of which every race of man partakes. Those who lived in accordance with Intellect are Christians, even though they are called godless, such as, among the Greeks, Socrates and Heraclitus and others like them.... Those who lived by Intellect, and those who so live now, are Christians, fearless and unperturbed."[10]

In recalling St. Justin's standpoint as a legitimate one for Christians to take with regard to adherents of other religions, the Bishop of Guildford thereby implicitly assents to its inescapable corollary, that the act of Redemption operates in other modes as well as the specifically Christian mode of the Passion. The contrary claim, that in a world subject to multiplicity the Divine Mercy, by definition Infinite, should be limited to one single effective act is in principle something that a metaphysician cannot readily accept, quite apart from the overwhelming factual evidence against it. Admittedly the majority cannot be sacrificed to a minority; but certain claims which may have "worked" in the past are of an increasingly dubious value for the majority while being lethal to the intellectual minority. There are Christians for whom the Bhagavat-Gita comes next to the Gospels and the Psalms as their most revered book; and this Hindu scripture bears a most eloquent and irrefutable witness to a redeeming Divine Incarnation other than Jesus in the person of Krishna and, by extension, of other Hindu Avataras, including the Buddha.

As Frithjof Schuon remarks:

Every exoteric doctrine is in fact characterized by a disproportion between its dogmatic demands and its dialectical guarantees; for its demands are absolute as deriving from the Divine Will and therefore also from Divine Knowledge, whereas its guarantees are relative, because they are independent of this Will and based, not on Divine Knowledge, but on a human point of view, that of reason and sentiment. For instance, Brahmins are invited by Christian missionaries to abandon completely a religion that has lasted for several thousand of years, one that has provided the spiritual support of innumerable generations and has produced flowers of wisdom and holiness down to our times. The arguments that are produced to justify this extraordinary demand are in no wise logically conclusive, nor do they bear any proportion to the magnitude of the demand; the reasons that the Brahmins have for remaining faithful to their spiritual patrimony are therefore infinitely stronger than the reasons by which it is sought to persuade them to cease being what they are. The disproportion, from the Hindu point of view, between the immense reality of the Brahmanic tradition and the insufficiency of the religious counter arguments is such as to prove quite sufficiently that had God wished to submit the world to one religion only, the arguments put forward on behalf of this religion would not be so feeble, nor those of certain so-called "infidels" so powerful; in other words, if God were on the side of one religious form only, the arguments put forward on behalf of this religion would be such that no man of good faith would be able to resist it.[11]

The title of this chapter makes the many references to Frithjof Schuon inevitable because his writings lead the way in giving the mind its due in respect of religion. Not that they are limited to the mind, any more than the mind, in the context of "with all thy mind", can be limited to itself, since to be fully operative its higher reaches depend directly on the heart. It is to the mind, to the intermediary intellective faculties, and to the heart that Frithjof Schuon's writings are above all addressed. To avoid giving a false impression, however, it must be added, as regards the soul, that while demolishing certain outworn human arguments which have in the past served the cause of "with all thy soul", he puts other arguments of a higher order in their place. Few writers, if any, have so clearly demonstrated the importance of sacred art in this respect. And who in recent centuries has written so profoundly and unmoralistically about the necessity of virtue?

To the passage written for Christians in affirmation of the validity of Hinduism, let us add the following affirmation of Islam:

> .....that God could have allowed a religion that was merely the invention of a man to conquer a part of humanity and to maintain itself for more than a thousand years in a quarter of the inhabited world, thus betraying the love, faith, and hope of a multitude of sincere and fervent souls—this is contrary to the Laws of the Divine Mercy, or in other words, to those of Universal Possibility.[12]

To consider now the limitations of Muslim exoterism, it must be remembered that from its stronghold of finality as the last religion of this cycle of time, Islam, unlike Judaism and Christianity, can afford to be generous to other religions. Moreover its position in the cycle confers on it something of the function of summer-up, which obliges it to mention with justice what has preceded it, or at the least to leave an open door for what it does not specifically mention.

Verily We have sent messengers before thee.[13] *About some of them have We told thee, and about some have We not told thee* (XL, 78).

We may quote also:

Verily the Faithful[14] and the Jews and the Sabians[15] and the Christians—whoso believeth in God and the Last Day and doeth deeds of piety—no fear shall come upon them neither shall they grieve (V, 69).

There is a place for both Judaism and Christianity within the Islamic civilization, and Muslims are obliged to protect the synagogues and churches and other Jewish and Christian sanctuaries. It was a calamity for Spanish Jews when the Christians conquered Spain.

It has to be admitted, however, that the authorities of Islam have been no less ready than their counterparts in other religions to risk "with all thy mind" for the sake of "with all thy soul and with all thy strength." Muslims have been encouraged to believe, and the majority have been only too eager to believe, that Islam has superseded all other religions and that it is therefore the sole truly valid religion on earth. But, however absolute the claims of Muslim theologians and jurisprudents may be, they are shown in fact to be relative by the tolerance which Islam makes obligatory towards Judaism and Christianity. Taken with that "grain of salt"—though few are fully conscious of it—the claims in question are not necessarily unpalatable to the intelligence, and are not bound to prevent an intellectual from loving God with all his mind, provided he remain within the walls of the Islamic civilization, which stop him from seeing the full implications of this exclusivism.

But once outside these walls, the situation is different. The most that a sound intelligence can accept are the claims which naturally result from the fact that Islam represents the most recent Divine intervention upon earth. But these claims, though considerable, are relative, not absolute;[16] and a Muslim intellectual in the modern world will not find peace of mind except by assenting to this. It should not however be difficult for him to do so, for a glance at those passages of the Qur'ān on which the theologians' exclusivism is based shows that the verses in question call for a deeper and more universal interpretation than is generally given.

One of these passages is the following:

> *He it is who hath sent His Messenger with guidance and the religion of Truth, that He may make it prevail over all religion, though the idolaters be averse* (IX, 33).

/This verse can be given a narrower or a wider interpretation. Its more immediate meaning is clearly the narrower one: the *Messenger* is Muḥammad, *the religion of Truth* is the Quranic message and the *idolaters* are the pagan Arabs and certain other pagans. To the words *that He may make it prevail over all religion* must be added "in your part of the world."/

Whatever the disadvantages of modern education, it serves to implant a more global concept of world history and geography than is normally held by members of traditional civilizations which tend, as we have seen, to be "aloof" and "introspective." The wider knowledge is a mixed blessing, but where it exists it must be taken into account. An intelligent Muslim, living in the modern world, is bound to realize sooner or later, suddenly or gradually, not only that the Quranic message has not been made to *prevail over all religion* in a wider sense, but also that Providence itself is directly responsible for the "shortcoming." The shock of this realization may shatter his belief, unless he is enabled to understand that the verse in question has a wider significance. In the narrower sense, *all religion* can only be taken to mean "all religion in your part of the world, except for those who are already Jews or Christians." But if *all religion* be interpreted in an absolute sense, and if *idolaters* be made to include such people as the Germans and Celts, many of whom were still pagan at the outset of Islam, then *the religion of Truth* must also be given its widest application, and the words "once again" must be understood (i.e. *He it is who hath sent once again His Messenger...*), for the Divinity has sent messengers before, and never with anything other than *the religion of Truth*. These last four words, like the term Islam itself, can be taken in a universal sense, to include all true religion. /The Qur'ān makes it clear that the religions of Adam, Noah, Abraham, Moses and Jesus may be called "Islam" in its literal meaning of "submission to God." /In this sense Islam may be said to have been made to *prevail over all religion*.[17] But in its narrower sense Islam has only been allowed to *prevail over all religion* in a limited part of the world. It is now fourteen hundred years since the revelation of the Qur'ān and Providence has allowed non-Quranic modes of *the religion of Truth* to remain as barriers to the Quranic message in more than half the globe.

In the same context, verses affirming that Muḥammad has been sent *for all people* (XXXIV, 28) have to be understood in a less monopolizing way than they have been throughout the centuries by Muslims with little or no general knowledge about other religions and their distribution. /What the Qur'ān tells us here is that Islam, unlike Judaism or Hinduism, is a world religion. /But it is not denying that Buddhism and Christianity are also world religions, that is, open to everybody, at least in principle. /These last words are important, for *God doth what He will* (II, 253), and our only means of knowing His Will in this respect are by the results.[18] With regard to the world as it has been in its geographical distribution of peoples for the last two thousand years, it will not escape the notice of an observant Muslim any more than an observant Christian that there is, spatially speaking, a certain sector in which Providence has worked wonders for Buddhism and done relatively little for either Christianity or Islam. The same Muslim will also notice that there is another sector in which Providence has worked wonders for Christianity and done little for the other world religions; and the fact that between these two sectors there is a third in which Islam has been favoured beyond all other religions will not be enough to exonerate him from changing this perspective. For if, as he had been led to believe, God had truly wished Islam (in the narrower sense) to spread over the whole world, why did He construct such impregnable barriers to it in so vast an area?[19]

To take the nearest example, Providence was putting an end to paganism in England at the very time when the Qur'ān was being revealed. *The religion of Truth*, in its Christian mode, was being made to *prevail over all religion*, although the idolaters were averse; and since a Divine intervention is never mediocre, Christianity was being established on the firmest foundations, so that not even the Quranic message, at the height of the power of the Islamic civilization, could come near to prevailing against it. And yet it would have been easy for Providence to have waited a few years and converted England to the new religion instead of setting up there such a resistance to it. The answer to the "problem", if anyone considers it to require an answer, lies in the following verse, which many consider to be among the last Revelations received by the Prophet and which in any case belongs to the period which marks the close of his mission. As such it coincides with a cyclic moment of extreme significance—the last "opportunity"[20] for a direct message to be sent from Heaven to earth during what remains of this cycle of time. Many of the last Quranic Revelations are concerned with completing and perfecting the new religion. But this verse is a final and lasting message for mankind as a whole. The Qur'ān expressly addresses the adherents of all the different orthodoxies on earth; and no message could be more relevant to the age in which we live and, in particular, to the mental predicament of man in these latter days.

For each of you We have appointed a law and a way. And if God [21] *had so willed He would have made you one people. But (He hath willed it otherwise) that He may put you to the test in what He has given you.* [22] *So vie with one another in good works. Unto God will ye be brought back, and He will inform you about that wherein ye differed* (V, 48).

CHAPTER FOUR

What is the Spiritual Significance of Tears and of Laughter?

In both these spontaneous overflowings of the body the material realm is transcended. But at their highest level, which is indicated here by the word "spiritual", the psychic plane is also largely surpassed.

The body is necessarily endowed with various means of escape from itself. Some of these are merely at its own level, not to speak of that which, by the very fact of its separation, necessarily sinks from being a living substance to a dead substance. But at the same time the escape in itself, as such, can in varying degrees afford access to a higher plane of existence. In the vast majority of cases however the access does not rise higher than the psychic plane, and therefore does not come within the scope of our present theme. Otherwise expressed, to revert to our title, the word "spiritual" must be given its full exclusive value. There can be tears of pain which affect both body and soul, and there are tears of anger or of sorrow or a general unhappiness which give a certain relief to the soul.

As to what might be called the central means of escape from the body, namely orgasm, which can have a significance at every level, enough has been written about it by Frithjof Schuon to absolve us from intruding upon what he has so well expressed.[1] Also in connection with the scope of this chapter, but from a very different angle, it must be clearly understood that the words "religious" and "spiritual" are by no means synonymous. The domain of the Spirit may be said to coincide with the *Paradiso* of Dante's epic, but it lies beyond the *Purgatorio*. Without belittling the extreme importance of tears of contri-

44

tion, they can and must be relegated to their own degree in the hierarchy of the faculties. The Spirit, by definition, can have no cause for repentance. Gratitude on the other hand is an essential aspect of the Spirit, and it can therefore be affirmed that although not all tears of thanksgiving are up to that level, some such tears may indeed be described as spiritual. When it is said in Christianity that he or she is blessed with *dona lacrimarum*, the gift of tears, this privilege is generally considered to be the outward sign of a venerable degree of spirituality.

Very relevant in this context is a passage from the Qur'ān addressed to the Prophet telling him as regards men of other religions that he would find among Christians the nearest to himself and to his Muslim followers. *Thou shalt find that the nearest in affection to believing Muslims are those who say: "Verily we are Christians." That is because they have amongst them priests and monks, and because they are not proud. And when they hear that which hath been revealed unto the Messenger thou seest their eyes overflowing with tears at their recognition of the Truth. They say: "Our Lord, we believe, so inscribe us amongst those who bear witness to the Truth"* (V, 82-3).

To take another extremely different example of truly spiritual tears which are likely in this particular case to be Christian though they need not necessarily be so, anyone who comes out of the National Gallery in Trafalgar Square has clearly to move in some direction or other. One possibility is to make for the Strand by the nearest way, past the church of St. Martin-in-the-Fields, and then, in the Strand itself, past the churches of St. Mary le Strand and St. Clement Dane. It must have happened more than once over the last hundred years or so that the walker's eyes have suddenly filled with tears, not tears of vexation at the total lack of uplift in the Renaissance, Baroque and Classical churches that have just been passed, but tears of wonderment and gratitude at the beauty of the Law Courts by which one is rather suddenly faced at the east end of the Strand. They were built towards the end of the nineteenth century by a man named George Street, in thirteenth century Gothic style, no doubt under the influence of Augustus Pugin who had played a large

part in the rebuilding of the Palace of Westminster, often referred to as the Houses of Parliament. The old Palace had been
burned down in 1834, but the new Palace was not finished until
1850. We are in fact immensely indebted to Pugin and Street
and others like them for having seen beyond any doubt that
since the Divine gift of Gothic, Western Christendom has not
been endowed with any subsequent gift from Heaven in the
domain of architecture. In other words, no post-Gothic architecture can rank as sacred art. It is indeed tragic that when old
St. Paul's was burnt down in the seventeenth century fire of
London, the almost unanimous wishes of Londoners that the
new St. Paul's should be built in the same style were totally
disregarded.

To take another somewhat equivalent example to that of the
Law Courts, but less sudden and more spectacular, an experience which must many times have brought tears to sensitive
eyes, a walk along Victoria Street in the direction of the river
brings the walker eventually within sight of Westminster Abbey. The little church of St. Margaret stands beside it, and in
the background to both, on the bank of the Thames, is the Palace of Westminster. I cannot help thinking that the following
anecdote would have given much pleasure to Pugin, as also to
Street and to others like them. I once had the good fortune to
visit the Abbey with Frithjof Schuon, and as we were drawing
near, one of those who were with us inadvisably chose to say,
pointing to the Palace of Westminster: "But that is only pseudo-
Gothic", whereupon Schuon said: "There is no such thing as
pseudo-Gothic; Gothic is Gothic, and that is one of the most
beautiful palaces I have ever seen."

Needless to say, many tears must have been shed throughout the centuries by those who have been fortunate enough to
be gazing spell-bound at Durham Cathedral, at Lincoln Cathedral, at York Minster and during the Middle Ages, at Fountains
Abbey and the many other wonders that were destroyed at the
so-called Reformation. Or to take a somewhat different example, those who from some vantage point on one of the gentle
slopes of open country which come remarkably near to the capi-

tal city of the county of Wiltshire, will have seen at one point a group of trees growing up from the green fields, and from another point the spire of Salisbury Cathedral "growing up" also amid the greenery as if to demonstrate the profound truth that sacred art can never strike an alien note amid the beauties of nature for the simple reason that the Artist of both is fundamentally One and the Same. It is not by false modesty that in the various traditional civilizations throughout the world so much sacred art is deliberately anonymous.

"Sacred art is made as a vehicle for spiritual presences. It is made at the same time for God, for angels and for man. Sacred art helps man to find his own centre."[2] We may conclude from this profound definition by Frithjof Schuon that sacred art is an invitation held out to man that makes it possible for him to adopt a divine or at least an angelic standpoint. Moreover the helping of man to find his centre brings us once again to the notion of escape, for man's centre is supernatural, beyond the strictly human plane. It is no doubt relevant to mention here, as we have done elsewhere, that in all esoterisms, that is, in the innermost aspects of the different religions, there is bound to be mention of what is called "the eye of the Heart." This is the centre that sacred art helps man to find; and a centre transcends the whole periphery around it, abruptly and in all directions, that is, in exaltation, in profundity and in inwardness. It is this centre, precisely, which was lost by man at his fall.

So far we have only considered the visual arts, and only one aspect of these; but before we enlarge our scope, let us point out that our theme obliges us to follow Frithjof Schuon's refusal to accept as sacred art only that which strictly conforms to the canons of liturgical art, and to insist on a twofold sacred art, by reason of the necessity of including, in the domain of the sacred, all that is a manifestation of the Divine Beauty, for That is always the supreme prompter of tears.

Among the visual arts not yet mentioned are the traditional arts of painting and statuary, each of which has produced unsurpassable wonders in its own marvellously original way, for example the Taoist landscape paintings of China and Japan, the statues of Buddhism, Hindu painting of the Kangra school, the icons of Eastern and Western Christianity, of which the Islamic equivalent is to be found in the sacred art of Qur'ān calligraphy and illumination.[3] We are also conscious, in the background, of wonders bequeathed to us by no longer operative traditions such as the statues and wall paintings of ancient Egypt.

To consider another unsurpassable mover to tears, the great Algerian Shaykh Aḥmad al-ʿAlawī, about whom I wrote my book *A Sufi Saint of the Twentieth Century*, is recorded as having said: "Music is not crippled by the dry bones of words. Liquid and flowing like a stream, it carries us into the presence of God." But lest this should be taken in an exclusive sense, and being himself a poet, he would certainly have welcomed what his disciple, Frithjof Schuon, said in an unpublished text, about the immense power of rhythm. He is speaking directly about the ritual dances of Sufism; but if we may venture to be explicit where he is implicit, it could be said that rhythm is a miraculous bridge between movement and repose, and amongst other things it is able to confer upon "the dry bones of words" the power and privileges of music. We might add that another somewhat analogous gift from Heaven, in the numerical domain, are the sacred numbers which act as a bridge between multiplicity and unity.

Needless to say, in addition to the great outer world, to virgin nature, that is, to all that is left of the world as it was created, uncontaminated by human civilisation, there is also the sacred art of the microcosm, man as he was first created in our first ancestors and also, since the fall of man, in the messengers who have been sent to establish the religions, each of whom is a great work of sacred art.

We have already mentioned virgin nature in connection with the arts of landscape painting and also in a reminder that in all truly sacred art, whether man be involved or whether it exists independently of human participation, the Artist is always One and the Same. But before we leave this context, let us quote the following verses from the Qur'ān. Islam is insistent that there can be no true piety without wonderment at the marvellous signs of God which surround us on all sides in this world, but which an increasing majority of people take for granted. Nonetheless there are always some who take them for what they truly are or, otherwise expressed, who are more or less conscious of the Divine Archetype in which the signs are rooted and which they manifest in this earthly plane. This consciousness is a mode of wonderment, and wherever wonderment is granted it may be accompanied by those tears which are at the level of our theme, though their absence cannot be said to diminish the escape that wonderment is in itself.

As regards the following quotation, it must be remembered that the Revelation is directly addressed to the Arabs in whose language it is, whence the opening mention of camels which were then the Arabs' best means of travel, that is, of having an extended view of the world which surrounds us. *Will they not behold the camels how they are created? And the firmament, how it is raised aloft? And the mountains, how they are established? And the earth, how it is spread?* (LXXXVIII, 17-20).

Macrocosm and microcosm, great outer world with all that it contains, and small world of each single human being. Both these worlds are made in the image of God, and they are therefore analogous; but man has fallen whereas the world he lives in remains as it was created except insofar as fallen man has desecrated it. God has however promised that "the earth shall not be found lacking in forty men whose hearts are as the heart of the friend of God," that is, Abraham. There are also the other messengers of God, each a model of human perfection. Moreover for the people of each particular religion the founder of that religion is still mysteriously present with them, enough to be wondered at by those who are capable of wonderment.

In other words, the microcosm in its primordial perfection together with the macrocosm are both works of art from the same Artist. In the Qur'ān God says to Moses: *O Moses I have fashioned thee for Myself* (XX, 41); and the same is implied in another verse in which God says to Muḥammad: *Verily of an immense magnitude is thy nature* (LXVIII, 4).

Just as the various macrocosmic wonders of nature depend for their fullest revelation on certain conditions such as those of season, climate and time of day, so also a microcosmic work of sacred art, while retaining always its perfection, may make himself or herself deliberately or instinctively transparent, that is, more evocative of wonderment, on certain occasions than on others, just as providentially the beholders' sense of transparency may be sharpened.

Most of our readers will know that the New Testament is rich in quoting utterances or relating acts whereby we are compelled to marvel, with or without tears, at the Divine "work of art" that every founder of a religion, in this case Christianity, necessarily is. It goes without saying that a Divine message is irresistible. God does what He wishes, and if He sees the need to establish a new religion He will do so despite the opposition which is implicit in that very need itself.

To take as an example the outset itself, we may quote: "And Jesus was walking by the shore of the sea, and he came upon two fishermen who were casting in their nets; and he said unto them: 'Leave your nets and follow me, and I will make you fishers of men.'"[4] For another example, spoken not long before the Ascension, there are the words he spoke to "doubting Thomas" when he showed him the stigmata: "Thomas, because thou hast seen me thou hast believed; blessed are they that have not seen and yet have believed."[5]

Far less well known, but particularly relevant to our theme, is an incident from the life of the Prophet Muḥammad, which needs some preliminary explanation. Having received from Heaven the order to preach the monotheistic religion of Islam to the now polytheistic people of Mecca, and having thereby incurred the hostility of almost all the men of power in that city to the point of being in danger of losing his life, he was guided by the Archangel Gabriel to leave his beloved birthplace and home, and to accept the invitation of a group of converts to go and live in the oasis of Yathrib some eleven camel days to the North. These converts were men of considerable standing in Yathrib, and it was not long before the new Prophet had become something like a king. The most closely inhabited part of the oasis where he was taken to live was known as "the city", in Arabic *al-madinah*, and to this day it still bears the name Medina. Meantime more and more converts to Islam were migrating from Mecca and elsewhere in order to be with him.

The polytheists of Mecca, foreseeing that their way of life might soon be endangered, sent more than one powerful army against Medina but without any success, and finally, thanks to the continued stream of converts from Mecca, and alliances with neighbouring tribes, the Prophet was able to set out himself for Mecca with an army which he knew they would not be able to resist. He did not however make known to his men their final destination but kept it a secret except from one or two of his closest Companions, and the powerful hostile Arab tribe of *Hawāzin* to the East of Mecca assumed that they were the object of attack, and they mustered a large army of defence.

Polytheism was fostered in Arabia by three shrines of the so-called goddesses *al-ᶜUzzah*, *Manāt* and *al-Lāt*. The second of these shrines which was nearest to Medina had already been destroyed, and from Mecca, soon after his arrival, the Prophet ordered the destruction of the shrine of *al-ᶜUzzah*. Meantime, in Mecca itself, hundreds of men and women, including some who had been his worst enemies, came and pledged allegiance to him and entered Islam.

There still remained however the shrine of the third goddess, *al-Lāt*, and this was on the territory of the tribe of *Hawāzin* who were determined to protect it and who, as we have seen, had already mustered an army to protect themselves; and about two weeks after the Prophet's army had entered Mecca, the news came that *Hawāzin*, having decided that attack was the best means of defence, were already on the march against Mecca with an army considerably larger than that which the Prophet had brought from Medina.

The Prophet set out immediately from Mecca to meet them, and in addition to his own troops were hundreds of Meccans who had only just entered Islam in varying degrees of sincerity, together with others who had not yet made up their minds but who felt obliged to defend their city against the attack.

The leader of *Hawāzin* had insisted that they should bring with them, behind their army, their women and children, whose presence, so he said, would inspire the men to fight all the better. At first, owing to a cunning strategy on their part, the battle went in their favour, but the Prophet and those closest to him were able to stand their ground, and taking a handful of pebbles he threw them at the enemy with the prayer: "Thy promise, O Lord." This promise was that for those who stood firm in battle God would send down a thousand angels to put the enemy to flight. The tide of the battle suddenly changed, and some of the enemy took refuge in the walled city of Ṭā'if, while others took to the hills. The *Hawāzin* women and children were all made captive and the rest of the booty amounted to many thousands of camels and about twice the number of sheep and goats.

For a few days the Prophet laid siege to Ṭā'if but then he decided that other issues were more urgent at that moment. But as they marched away the plea of one of his troops that he should put a curse on the men behind the walls drew from him its opposite, that is, the prayer that God would give them to him, and he knew that his prayer would be answered. Meantime the question of the captives had to be considered and the distribution of the spoils.

The Prophet had received recently a Revelation which added another category of persons, in addition to the poor and the needy, who were entitled to receive gifts from the funds that were accumulated from alms and from the spoils of battle. This category was defined as *those whose hearts are to be reconciled*, and the Prophet saw clearly the extreme relevance of this new message from Heaven with regard to the battle they had recently won. A number of those Meccans who had fought on their side and had fought well, were not yet Muslims, and as to the hundreds of Meccan men and women who had entered Islam only now, the fact that they had not done so before clearly placed some of them in the category *those whose hearts are to be reconciled.* But what the Prophet saw with immediate clarity was by no means clear to all his troops.

Apart from relatively new converts to Islam from tribes neighbouring on Yathrib, the main part of the army that had marched with him to Mecca consisted of men of the oasis itself and those Meccans who, since his arrival in Medina, had entered Islam and had left their homes in order to be with him. The Meccans were known as "the Emigrants"; their hosts, the men of the oasis, were known as "the Helpers." With regard to the spoils of war it was easy for the Emigrants to enter into the Prophet's generosity towards "those whose hearts are to be reconciled" because they themselves were Meccans, and many of those who now received rich gifts from the spoils of war were their own relatives. But the Helpers were not Meccan, and not a few of them were exceedingly poor. When the spoils were divided it was decided that each man who had fought against the men of *Hawāzin* had the right to receive four camels or their equivalent in sheep and goats; but this was nothing compared with the hundred camels which were now given to some of those whose hearts needed to be reconciled. Worse still, a rumour was started and spread throughout the Helpers that the Prophet, himself a Meccan, did not intend to return with them to Medina, now that he would once more be welcome in the beloved city of his birth and upbringing. When the sense of injustice rose high amongst them, one of their chief men decided that it was his duty to inform the Prophet, who told him to gather all the Helpers together so that he could speak to them. When they were ready he went to them and having given praise and thanks to God he said: "Men of the Helpers, word hath come to me that ye are deeply moved against me in your souls. Did I not find you erring, and God guided you, poor and God enriched you, enemies each of the other and God reconciled your hearts?" "Yea indeed", they answered. "God and His Messenger are most bountiful and most gracious." "Will ye not retort against me?" he said. "How should we retort?" they asked, in some perplexity. "If ye wished", he answered, "ye might say unto me, and say truthfully, and be believed: 'Thou didst come unto us discredited and we credited thee, forlorn and we helped thee, an outcast and we took thee in, destitute and we comforted thee.' O Helpers, are ye stirred in your souls about the things of this world whereby I have reconciled men's hearts, when you yourselves I have entrusted unto your Islam? Are ye not well content, O Helpers, that the people take with them their sheep and their camels, and that ye take with you the Messenger of God unto your homes? If all men but the Helpers went one way, and the Helpers another, I would go the way of the Helpers. God have Mercy on the Helpers, and on their sons, and on their sons' sons." They wept until their beards were wet with their tears, and with one voice they said: "We are well content with the Messenger of God as our portion and our lot."[6]

It might be argued, against the inclusion here of our last quotation, that these tears were shed simply in relief that the rumours had proved to be false, and that the Prophet was not intending to settle once again in the city of his birth, but to continue to live with them in their city. In other words, it might be argued that these tears were purely at the psychic level, and that as such they are not relevant to our theme. I would readily admit that they were partly at the psychic level; but I would insist that they were largely prompted by an exceptionally close and clear vision that God had at that moment granted them of the great beauty of one of His works of sacred art, a perfect man made in His image to be one of His Messengers, and as such at the level of primordial man, the microcosmic equivalent of the great outer world of virgin nature, the world of plains, forests, hills, mountains, springs, rivers and lakes, the macrocosm of earth bounded by sky and ocean.

In the context of tears, it must not be forgotten that there are also tears of laughter, and that laughter itself is akin to tears as an escape from the body to the psychic level and also to what transcends that level. It could no doubt be said that as mankind degenerates there is an increasing amount of laughter which barely escapes from the bodily domain. Many restaurants today are noisy with raucous laughter which is uttered without any motive behind it other than the desire to gain the reputation of being "good company." The spontaneous laughter of children is a refreshing contrast, and it is sometimes accompanied by tears. Over the years I have heard it said more than once: "We laughed till we cried." It would no doubt be inadvisable to say that such laughter can never rise above the psychic level, for "the Spirit bloweth where it listeth", and human happiness, which is always in any case a manifestation of the Divine Felicity, can be on rare occasions, by especial grace, an exceptionally direct manifestation of its Archetype.

To refer once again to the Prophet Muḥammad, it is recorded[7] that on one occasion, by a sudden unexpected incident which seemed to him overwhelmingly humorous, he was plunged into laughter which made it impossible for him to speak.

The situation was briefly as follows. One morning in the days which followed the successful campaign of Khaybar, ᶜUmar who was one of the Prophet's closest Companions, came to visit him, and as he approached he heard the sound of women's voices raised to a pitch which he considered to be unseemly in the Prophet's presence. The women were moreover, like himself, of Quraysh, that is, of the Emigrants, which confirmed his opinion that they were learning bad ways from the women of Medina, who for generations had been less restrained and more self-assertive than the women of Mecca. The Prophet hated to refuse a request, as well they knew, and they were now asking him, with some insistence, to give them various garments which had come to him as part of the spoils of war. There was a curtain spread across part of the room, and when ᶜUmar's voice was heard, asking permission to enter, there was a sudden total silence and the women hid themselves behind the curtain with such speed that when ᶜUmar entered, with the Islamic greeting *as-Salāmu ᶜalaykum* (Peace be on you[8]), the Prophet was so speechless with laughter that he could not even answer ᶜUmar's greeting with its obligatory response *wa-ᶜalaykum as-Salām* (and on you be Peace). But it is not without significance with regard to the extent to which such laughter is traditionally treasured that on seeing the Prophet in this state ᶜUmar should have spontaneously said to him: "May God fill thy life with laughter, O Messenger of God!" When the Prophet was able to speak he said: "Wondrous it was how these women who were with me even now—how speedily upon hearing thy voice they were gone behind that curtain!" "It is rather thy right, not mine, that they should stand in awe of thee, not of me", said ᶜUmar. Then addressing the women, he said: "O enemies of your own souls, fear ye me, and fear ye not God's Messenger?" "It is even so," they said, "for thou art rougher and harsher than God's Messenger." "That is true," said the Prophet. But in a sense it was ᶜUmar who had the last word, for the Prophet added: "By Him in whose hand is my soul, if Satan found that thou wert travelling upon a certain path, he would choose to go himself by any other path but thine."[9]

Such laughter as that of the Prophet on this occasion, no doubt more often than not, is accompanied by tears, though they are not in fact mentioned in the text from which I have just been quoting. But I once had the immense privilege of seeing my own spiritual Master in a state of laughter clearly akin to that of the Prophet on the above mentioned occasion, and tears were by no means absent. It is well known in all esoterisms that the disciples of a Master seek to be in his presence not only in order to ask questions and to receive instructions but also and above all to benefit from the spiritual blessings which radiate from that presence. The Master has to defend himself to a considerable extent, since otherwise he would have no privacy. But on this occasion there was no question of undue intrusion, since I had been invited to spend the evening with him together with some other disciples who, like myself, had come from abroad to visit him. We were all however fully aware of the cause of the laughter, and within a few moments we had all been irresistibly drawn into it. We sat there, our bodies shaking and tears rolling down our cheeks. Not every one of us was absolutely speechless, and it lasted all the longer because one or two of us, including the Master himself, were able to gasp out remarks which gave new impetus to the laughter. The happiness that we experienced was indescribable. Needless to say, this is not a claim that what we felt was up to the degree of happiness that our Master personified in those precious moments. That, I do not doubt, was something of an overflow from the Divine Felicity Itself. Nonetheless, it could be that the Master had radiated something of that Felicity to us, or let us simply repeat "the Spirit bloweth where it listeth"; and speaking for myself I still treasure within me those moments of laughter, even to the point of being still able to relive something of them, although they took place more than half a century ago.

CHAPTER FIVE

What is the Spiritual Significance of Civilization?

My work in the Department of Oriental Manuscripts and Printed Books[1] at the British Museum often brought me into contact with Islamic institutions in London, the more so since I was myself the Museum Arabist in charge of the Arabic manuscripts and books. As a result I came to know fairly well the director of The Islamic Cultural Centre,[2] who one day sent me a message telling me that he had just received instructions from Egypt to choose an English Muslim to represent England at an International Islamic Congress which was being planned by the Azhar University in Cairo. He added: "Can you not obtain permission from The British Museum to attend this congress, all expenses paid?" My first impulse was to say no because of my dislike for congresses, that is, dislike of the obligation to sit and listen to talk after talk, many of which are likely to be without interest. Moreover and above all, as will I think be deductible from the previous chapters of this book, I am not the sort of person that is qualified to "represent England", because I am deliberately "out of touch" with people. I knew that reporters would come and ask me how many Muslims live in England and how many of these are recent converts, and I neither know nor want to know what is the answer. Socially speaking, I want to be left alone to lead a quiet life, and I have always made a point of living, if possible, in an "out of the way" place so that my privacy will be less in danger of being invaded.

On the other hand, as the result of having been for over twelve years a lecturer on English Literature (mainly Shakespeare) at the University of Cairo, I had been accustomed to visit the tombs of the great Saints who are buried in the older parts of the city, and I am always happy to revisit them. /Cairo also has in it perhaps more mosques of exquisite beauty, both large and small, than any other city in the world. /I knew also that the National Library of Egypt has an unsurpassed collection of marvellously illuminated manuscripts of the Qur'ān, a collection which is as far as I can tell only equalled by one or two collections in Istanbul and in Iran. Moreover the director of my department in the British Museum encouraged me to go, and obtained permission for me to accept the invitation, which I finally did.

The congress was divided into two groups, that is, the representatives of Islamic countries in the Near and Middle East, and the representatives of Islamic communities in other countries which had no specifically Islamic status. There were two sessions each day, and about six speakers were listed, with time for questions and answers after each talk. We all met together for meals except for breakfast which we had in the various hotels that we were lodged in. The congress itself was held in a spacious building on the edge of the East bank of the Nile. Wherever we went, our eyes were met by notices inscribed with the words, in massive Arabic letters, *Marḥaban bi 'ttaṭṭawwur*, that is, Welcome to Development. Evidently the organizers of the congress were bent on showing that they were "up to date."

One of the first talks was given by an elderly man from the Sudan, and it was based on a well known saying of the Prophet which, so the speaker claimed, had never been properly understood: "Islam began as a stranger and it will end as a stranger." The opening words are clearly a reference to the problems experienced by the Prophet in seeking to impose on the then polytheistic inhabitants of Arabia the alien idea of monotheism. But the speaker maintained that the second part of the saying had been misunderstood until this very day, and that he had come to give us its true meaning, which was that Islam would end by spreading over all those parts of the world which had hitherto remained alien to the Quranic message. In other words, that Islam would end as an alien by being adopted by aliens; and there were some implications that most of those present in the lecture hall were not doing enough to help this to come true.

When it was time for question and answer, I ventured to question the legitimacy of interpreting one saying of the Prophet without taking into consideration other sayings of his which were related to a similar theme, in this case the spiritual future of the world. I pointed out that the Prophet had not believed in what the modern world calls "progress", and I quoted several well known sayings of his, for example "No time will come upon you but will be followed by a worse" and "The best of my people are my generation, then they that come after them, then they that come after those." When I had finished I heard expressions of agreement with me from all sides, and then one or two came up to me and thanked me warmly for having said what I had said.

Later in the week an afternoon had been set aside for those who might wish to be taken outside Cairo to see certain examples of modern "developments" in some of the neighbouring districts. It did not sound at all interesting, and more than half the members of the congress declined to go. No lectures had been listed for that afternoon, and one of the officials came up to me, greatly to my surprise, and said that he had been told to ask me if I would give a talk. I said I would think it over, and let him know the next morning. I had not prepared anything, but I felt that the words "Welcome to Development" demanded some comment, and that was how I came to give the following talk which is here translated from the Arabic in which it was spoken.

We have heard many times during this conference the words "development" *(taṭawwur)* and "progress" *(taqaddum)* and "renewal" *(tajdīd)* and "renaissance" *(nahḍah)*, and perhaps it will not be a waste of time to pause and consider what they mean. "Development" means moving away from the principles, and although it is necessary to move a certain distance from the principles in order to make applications of them, it is of vital importance to remain near enough for contact with them to be fully effective. Development must therefore never go beyond a certain point. Our ancestors were acutely conscious that this danger point had been reached in Islam hundreds of years ago; and for us, who are so much further removed in time than they were from the ideal community of the Prophet and his companions, the danger is all the greater. How then shall we presume not to be on our guard? How shall we presume not to live in fear of increasing our distance from the principles to the point where development becomes degeneration? And indeed it may well be asked as regards most of what is proudly spoken of today as development: Is it not in fact degeneration?

As for "progress," every individual should hope to progress, and that is the meaning of our prayer *Guide us upon the way of transcendence*. The word "development" could also be used of individuals in the same positive sense. But communities do not progress; if they did, what community was better qualified to progress than the first Islamic community in all the impetus of its youth? Yet the Prophet said, "The best of my people are my generation, then they that come after them, then they that come after those." And we must conclude from the Qur'ān that with the passage of the centuries a general hardening of hearts is inevitable, for it says of one community, *a long length of time passed over them so that their hearts were hardened* (LVII, 16); and this same truth is to be understood also from what the Qur'ān says of the elect, that they are *many in the earlier generations and few in the later generations* (LVI, 13-4). The hope of communities must lie, not in "progress" or "development," but in "renewal," that is, restoration. The word "renewal" has been used so far throughout this conference mainly as a rather vague synonym of "development," but in its traditional, apostolic sense,[3] renewal is the opposite of development, for it means a restoration of something of the primordial vigour of Islam. Renewal is thus, for Muslims, a movement of return, that is, a movement in a backward rather than a forward direction.

As to "renaissance," it might in itself be used in the same sense as "renewal," but this word "renaissance" has very inauspicious associations, because the movement that is called the European Renaissance was nothing other, if we examine it carefully, than a renewal of the paganism of ancient Greece and Rome; and that same "renaissance" marked the end of the traditional Christian civilization and the beginning of this modern materialistic civilization. Is the "renaissance" that we now hear of as taking place in the Arab states different from that one, or is it of the same kind?

There is not one of us, whether he be Arab or non-Arab, who does not rejoice in the independence of the Arab states and of Islamic countries in general, and it was to be hoped that this independence would bring about a return to the noble civilization of Islam. But what do we see? We see the doors flung wide open to everything that comes from Europe and America without the slightest discrimination. It is not irrelevant to recall here that for us—and the same must be implicitly if not explicitly true of all religions—every earthly possibility falls into one of five categories, being either obligatory *(fard)*, strongly recommended *(mandūb)*, allowed *(mubāh)*, strongly discouraged *(makrūh)*, or forbidden *(harām)*. It is against the second and fourth of these that a subversive movement will direct its efforts, at any rate to begin with, for since they are less absolute than the first and the fifth, it is easier to break through their defences. And it is to be noticed that the terms *mandūb* (strongly recommended) and *makrūh* (strongly discouraged) have changed their significance. Thus, in the eyes of the champions of this "renaissance" that we are now supposed to be enjoying, what is to be "strongly discouraged" is everything that is left of the Islamic civilization in the way of *sunnah*[4] such as wearing the turban and not shaving off the beard, whereas what is "strongly recommended" is everything that comes from the West. It may well be that only a very few actually go so far as to say that this or that is to be discouraged because it belongs to the civilization of our pious ancestors or that a thing is to be recommended because it comes from the West. But to judge by the facts, one might imagine that such words were on every tongue, such thoughts in every head. And what is the result of this? The result is that the rising generation is more ignorant of the practices of the Messenger of God, and more cut off from those practices, than any generation that has come into existence since the dawn of Islam. How then shall we augur well of the present situation? And how shall we not shrink from the word "renaissance" as from an evil omen?

All this was foreseen by the Prophet. He said, "You will follow the ways of those who were before you[5] span for span and cubit for cubit until if they went down into the hole of a poisonous reptile you would follow them down." That descent is now taking place; and it is called development and progress.

More than one delegate has mentioned, during this conference, that Islam embraces the whole of life, and no one doubts this. But what is actually happening today in many if not most Islamic countries is that life is embracing Islam—embracing, no, for it is a stranglehold rather than an embrace! Life is crowding religion out, pushing it into a little corner, and stifling it more and more so that it can scarcely breathe.

And what is the remedy?

By way of answering this question, let us recollect certain outer aspects of our civilization—I mean, the Islamic civilization—aspects whose function was, and can be again, to act as a protective shell for the kernel, that is, for the religion itself. The fabric of our civilization is woven out of the example set by our Prophet; and particularly significant in this connection is the fact that his house was a prolongation of his mosque. Thus for twelve hundred years—and more in many Islamic countries—the houses of his people were prolongations of the mosques. The Muslim would take off his shoes when he entered his house just as he would take them off when he entered the mosque; he would sit in his house in the same manner as he sat in the mosque; he would put such ornaments on the walls of his house as he saw on the walls of the mosque; nor would he put in his house any ornaments that would not be suitable for the mosque. Thus he was continually surrounded by reminders of the spiritual dignity and spiritual responsibilities of man, and he dressed himself according to the same principles. His clothes were in keeping with the dignity of man's function as representative of God on earth, and at the same time they made it easy for him to perform the ablution, and they were in perfect conformity with the movements of the prayer. Moreover they were an ornament to the prayer, unlike modern European clothes which rob the movements of the prayer of all their beauty and impede them, just as they act as a barrier between the body and the ablution.

All that I have mentioned is outward, but the outward acts upon the inward, and a man's clothes and his home are the nearest of all things to his soul, and their influence on it is perpetual and therefore incalculably powerful. There can be no doubt that these outward things were one of the secrets of the depth of piety among Muslims, for twelve hundred years; and this brings us back to the saying that Islam embraces the whole of life. Thanks to the outer aspects of the Islamic civilization, the whole of life was in fact penetrated by religion, and I see no other remedy for our present religious crisis but a return to that noble civilization whose function it is to create a worthy setting for the spirit of the religion, a setting that makes relatively easy the fulfilment of our ritual obligations. Nor can the community dispense with the help of anything that makes this spiritual life easier, for *man was created weak*. But this return can be accomplished only by the widespread setting of examples.

Arabs, you are in the abode of Islam,[6] where after your independence you are free to do what you will, and we look toward you from outside that abode and place our hopes in you. Do not disappoint us.

All the talks I had attended so far had been politely applauded in varying degrees of enthusiasm. But when I came to the end of mine there was a dead silence, and I saw that some of the audience were weeping. Then the man who had been appointed as the leader of the non-Arab group of invitees to which I belonged, an elderly man from Senegal with a venerable appearance, rose to his feet and came towards me. He took my hand between his two hands, and without saying a word he just beamed into my face for two or three minutes. Then a much younger man—he was from the sub-continent— came up to me and said: *Kāna lāzim ani 'l-ḥaqqu yuqāāl* (It was necessary that the truth should be told). Then an Egyptian took me by the hand and said: *Jā'a mina 'l-qalbi fadakhala 'l-qulūb* (It came from the Heart, and it has entered the Hearts).

To revert once more to our chapter heading, let us end our answer to this question with a very relevant quotation from Frithjof Schuon: "In every religion some few centuries after its foundation, one sees a fresh flowering or a kind of second youth" (*In the Tracks of Buddhism*, p. 153). The "few centuries" he mentions give time for a theocratic civilization to develop as a result of the powerful radiation of the community of men and women who are devoutly practising the new religion. This in no sense contradicts the saying of the Prophet: "The best of my people are of my generation", nor its Christian equivalent, the saying of Christ to his Apostles: "Unto you it is given to know the mysteries of the kingdom of heaven, but unto them it is not given." Nonetheless, every theocratic civilization which has developed as a setting for each of the great religions of the world is indeed a wonderful thing, nor are the least of its wonders the sacred arts which developed in each of them as manifestations of different aspects of the Divine Beauty. But as we have seen, every such religion needs protection against a "renaissance" of the darkness which preceded it.

CHAPTER SIX

What is the Quranic Doctrine of the Afterlife and How is it Related to Sufism?

The Qur'ān makes it clear that there are many degrees in the hierarchy of the hereafter. But let us begin by considering the most decisive division which draws a line as it were between those who are saved and those who are not. To these two categories correspond the two main divisions of the hereafter namely Heaven (or Paradise) and Hell. What qualifies man for salvation? The answer is given by the Qur'ān immediately after the account of the Fall. *Then Adam received words from his Lord, Who relented unto him. Verily He is the Ever-Relenting, the All-Merciful... There shall come unto you from Me a guidance, and whoso followeth My guidance no harm shall come upon them neither shall they grieve* (II, 37-8. See also XLVI, 13-14). Thus the condition for salvation is following a guidance from God, that is, a religion revealed by God. Other verses show that the religion must be followed in full. But implicit in the names Ever-Relenting, Ever-Forgiving is allowance for difficulties. The Prophet said to his Companions: "Verily ye are in an age wherein if ye neglect one tenth of what is ordered ye shall perish. But hereafter a time will come when he who observeth one tenth of what is now ordered shall be saved."[1] The somewhat negative definition of salvation as escape from all harm and grief has a very positive ring in the Arabic and is complemented by the many Quranic descriptions of the joys of Paradise into which the saved are ushered by the Angels. All that they desire is given them there in lasting perfection. The Paradises are inevitably told of in terms of earthly joys. Some Christians have called the Quranic descriptions of Paradise materialistic; but the truth is that the real gardens, rivers, marriages are in the hereafter. Their likenesses that we know on earth are mere shadows or reflections. According to a Holy Tradition, that is, a Message spoken by God on the tongue of His Prophet, "I was a Hidden Treasure and I loved to be known, and so I created the world." The earthly state shares with the rest of creation the privilege of being a mirror in which God manifests Himself./Moreover it is the only mirror accessible to us in this life. So there is a constant refrain in the Qur'ān that we should meditate on the wonders of this world as Signs of God./

This world is precious inasmuch as it serves to manifest or reflect the Hidden Treasure. It is vanity inasmuch as it is no more than a reflection, and because it is, of all reflections, the faintest and most remote. The Paradises are incomparably nearer to the Treasure itself. They are in fact what they are through being in the very aura of the Treasure which is mirrored in them with incomparably greater clarity. So another constant Quranic refrain is the vanity of this life, its mediocrity, its frustrations, its brevity. *This lower life is naught but a pastime and a game and verily the abode of the hereafter, that, that is life, did they but know* (XXIX, 64). Both refrains, negative and positive about this world, are a basis for the Qur'ān's descriptions of Paradise. On the one hand the incomparable superiority of the hereafter is affirmed as above or as in the verse: *No soul knoweth what is secretly stored up for them of coolness of the eyes in reward for what they were wont to do* (XXX,17). But if the joys of Paradise are unimaginable they are not totally so because the joys of this life are there to give us an inkling of what to expect and what to hope for.

Give good tidings unto those who believe and do deeds of piety that verily they shall have gardens of Paradise watered by flowing rivers. Whenever they are given to eat of one of the fruits thereof they say: This is that which we were given aforetime, and they were given a likeness of it (II, 25). In a word the universe is a hierarchy of worlds one above the other, all reflections, growing fainter and fainter, of the Hidden Treasure which they were created to manifest. There would be no gardens in this world if it were not for the Gardens of Paradise, and no rivers if it were not for the Rivers of Paradise. And the Gardens and Rivers of Paradise themselves would vanish if the Hidden Treasure of the Divine Essence were not Itself the Garden of gardens and the River of rivers, and indeed all *will* vanish when the Treasure reabsorbs into Itself everything that it has manifested. Another Quranic refrain is *Do not all things return to God?* (XLII, 53) and *Unto God is the ultimate becoming* (XXIV, 42). Also relevant is the Divine Name The Inheritor (*al-Wārith*).

Perfect contentment is stressed in the Qur'ān as an essential characteristic of Paradise which means that that every blessed spirit has all that he or she is capable of desiring, but there is necessarily an immense hierarchy of Paradises to meet the vast difference of personal capacity to receive. *Behold how We have favoured some of them above others; and verily the hereafter is greater in degrees and greater in precedences* (XVII, 21). The Prophet said: "The people of Paradise will behold the high place that is above them even as they now behold the bright planet on the eastern or western horizon."[2]

Though the Paradises are numberless it is nonetheless possible to make divisions in the hierarchy. One Surah of the Qur'ān divides mankind into three groups which amounts to a two fold division of the saved (LVI, 7-9). The three are right, left and foremost. These last are said to be *many among the first and few among the last* (LVI, 13-14). According to the Prophet this means: "Many among the peoples of old and few among the later peoples." Those of the right are *many among the first and many among the last* (LVI, 39-40). They are given water to drink whereas the foremost drink wine and are further defined as *those brought near (muqarrabūn)*. When qualified by this epithet in Arabic the word "Angel" becomes "Archangel." The Prophet would thus sometimes speak of "my brother Gabriel." The nearness in question is, needless to say, nearness to God; and if it be asked "How near?" the fact that one of the Divine Names is "the Near" (*al-Qarīb*) signifies His Absolute Nearness. We may also quote to the same effect a somewhat later Meccan[3] Revelation: *We (God) are nearer to him (man) than his jugular vein* (L, 16). This answer recalls the term "The Supreme Identity" which was referred to in a previous chapter;[4] and in another early Meccan Surah the highest Saints are termed the slaves of God to indicate that they, like the Prophet himself, have fully realised their nothingness with regard to God, that very realisation being the absolute condition of their nearness.

In this same Sūrah a third group of the dwellers in Paradise is mentioned. These are named as the righteous (*al-Abrār*), and their aspirations towards the fullness of slavehood are made clear by the fact that the wine they are given to drink is flavoured at the Fountain of *Kāfūr* (LXXVI, 5) to which only the slaves have direct access. In another Sūrah their aspirations towards Nearness are analogously indicated by their being given to drink a draught which is flavoured with the musk of the Fountain of *Tasnīm* from which only the Near can drink directly (LXXXIII, 25-28). This brings us to Sufism, that is, to Islamic mysticism.

All mysticism is an anticipation of the next life already in this. Therefore the Quranic doctrine of the afterlife must coincide partly with the doctrine of Sufism. Verses about the highest saints express the aim and end of Sufism. The Qur'ān implicitly guarantees the existence of Sufism in each generation down to the present day.

If it be asked whether or not those who are saved go straight to Paradise after they die, the answer, as regards the vast majority, is no. But needless to say, for those few who, already in this life, have attained to the degree of nearness-slavehood, the paradisal gates are as it were already open. The same is promised in Islam also for martyrs (*shuhadā'*), those who are killed fighting in a Holy War, or who die of their wounds; and there is bound to be an equivalent to this, *mutatis mutandis*, in every religion. Nor can any religion be lacking in the equivalent of what the Prophet termed the Greater Holy War (*al-jihād al-akbar*), that is, the war against all that is negative in one's own soul; and this question is inextricably bound up with the universal saying: "Whoso dieth before his death, dieth not when he dieth."

It is legitimate to take the following verse of the Qur'ān as referring to both Holy Wars, the greater and the lesser. *Count not those who have been slain in the way of God as dead. Nay they are living, from their Lord they receive sustenance* (III, 169).

In most Muslim communities it is customary to send children to attend Qur'ān classes at a relatively early age when human memory is at its best, and some of these children are bound to show an aptitude for learning many passages by heart. It may even happen that one or two of these will ask their elders: "How can I become one of the foremost?" or "How can I be brought near?" The answer: "Lead a good life and perhaps after death you will be of those brought near" may satisfy most but not all. Some young souls will only accept the truest answer "Die before you die" and "In order to sprout a seed must be buried." The Qur'ān refers to this mystic death in the words: *Is he who was dead, and whom We brought to life, setting for him a light whereby he walketh among men, like unto him who is in darkness whence he cannot emerge?* (VI, 122). We have seen that the highest spiritual possibility is described as slavehood and nearness. The slaves drink at the Fountain of *Kāfūr*, the near at the Fountain of *Tasnīm*, but it must be understood that we are being told here of two aspects of the same Supreme State. What is the connection between these aspects? The perfection of slavehood is ritually enacted in the prostration before God which marks the profoundest moment of the canonical prayer. A verse of the Qur'ān says to the Prophet: *Prostrate thyself and draw near* (XCVI, 19) and the Prophet commented on this verse: "The slave is nearest his Lord when he is prostrate." Hence the secret identity of slavehood with nearness. All creatures are slaves and all are near because God Himself is Absolutely Near, *al-Qarīb*. But in the verses we are considering here those brought near and the slaves are they who have realised the truth of nearness and slavehood. The Righteous who are next in the hierarchy are those who aspire to the highest state. As we have seen, they drink wine that has been flavoured with camphor from the slaves' own Fountain of *Kāfūr* and wine that has been flavoured with musk from the near ones' own Fountain of *Tasnīm*. All Sufism is in a sense comprised in these two degrees of the hierarchy, the way itself being personified by the righteous, the aim and end by the slaves brought near, and the Quranic imagery helps us to understand what Ghāzalī meant when he defined Sufism as *Dhawq*, taste, that is direct perception in this life of the realities of the hereafter, symbolised in the Qur'ān by the food and drink of Paradise. He also added to his definition: he said "Taste and nearness"; there is no need to comment; and the fact that the Sufis always call themselves the Poor brings in the concept of slavehood. The slave is poor, Arabic *faqīr* (plural *fuqara'*), Persian *darvish*, whence the English word "dervish."

A question perhaps needs to be asked here: What awaits the vast majority of those who are saved between their death and their entry into Paradise? The Quranic answer is: *If ye avoid the great sins (kaba'ir) ye are forbidden We will wipe out your faults and cause you to enter with a noble entry* (IV, 31). "Wipe out" means bring to nothing. Purification is necessary, and therefore Purgatory is in the nature of things. But that is not all: there is mention of another category, "The Men on the Heights" who give their name to a chapter of the Qur'ān: *And on the heights are men... and they see Paradise and Hell. They call out to the people of Paradise: Peace be on you. They have not entered it yet, though they long to enter* (VII, 46). These are clearly those who have passed through Purgatory and are destined for Paradise but are not yet altogether ready. "The heights" seem to correspond to the top of the Mountain of Purgatory from which, in Dante's Divine Comedy, the purified souls enter Paradise. In Buddhism there is a similar waiting place: those not yet ready are enclosed in lotus buds at the edge of Paradise, buds which open gradually as the souls grow to full maturity. We are told no more about those waiting on the Heights but the necessity for this waiting place can be easily deduced from what

71

is said about Paradise itself. The Qur'ān makes it abundantly clear that among the greatest joys of the hereafter is the company of the blessed Spirits. To enter Paradise is a tremendous responsibility: each Spirit must be a source of wonderment and delight to the other Spirits. Therefore each must grow to perfection before entering, that is, he or she must grow to Sainthood.

The Qur'ān promises that each blessed Spirit will be given two Paradises (LV, 46). This is not explained but it is understandable that since man was created to be mediator between Heaven and Earth he has necessarily a dual nature which needs two Paradises to be fully satisfied. He is on the one hand concerned with the multiple things which immediately surround him and on the other hand he is concerned with God, we might say with the Transcendent. The Surah of the Qur'ān in question mentions two pairs of Paradises, one pair higher than the other. According to commentators[5] the highest of these four Paradises is not a Paradise in the ordinary sense but is no less than the Hidden Treasure, and it is named "*Riḍwān*" or "The Paradise of the Essence." Below it is "The Paradise of the Spirit." Together these two Paradises constitute the hereafter of the highest Saints. This corresponds to the Prophet's definition of his own hereafter, "The Meeting with my Lord and Paradise." *Riḍwān* is difficult to translate: it means God's acceptance of a Saint, His taking him to Himself and whelming him in His Presence. It expresses the highest spiritual possibility and so when speaking of the Saints in Islam it is customary to add "May God give him, or her, His *Riḍwān*." "Good pleasure" is too weak in this connection. We may quote the following Quranic verse: *God hath promised the believers, the men and the women Gardens that are watered by flowing rivers wherein they shall dwell immortal; and Riḍwān from God is greater. That is the supreme achievement* (IX, 72). Let us quote also a verse which addresses one who is destined for the highest state: *O thou soul which art at peace return unto thy Lord with gladness that is thine in Him and His in thee. Enter thou among My Slaves; enter thou My Paradise* (LXXXIX, 27-30).

There is here again the same duality. "My Paradise" is the Divine Presence Itself, the Paradise of the Essence, for it is God who is speaking. The entry among the slaves refers to the Paradise of the Spirit, "slaves" being used here of the highest Saints who alone are allowed to drink as we have seen at the Fountain of Camphor, "*Kāfūr.*" As to the lower pair of Paradises, their relationship is analogous at its own level: here the higher Paradise is concerned with what is often called "Beatific Vision" whereas the lower is concerned with multiple joys on every side. But this mention of two pairs of Paradises must on no account be taken in a limitative sense, as if there were only four Paradises altogether. The Revelation is here simply affirming a hierarchy. In verse after verse the Qur'ān affirms the hereafter's immensity and freedom from limitation as compared with all that is most marvellous in this lower life.

In connection with the already quoted verse of the Qur'ān which tells us that in later times those who are truly spiritual will be few in number (LVI, 14), it is not irrelevant to mention that throughout the Qur'ān when we come to the words *aktharu 'n-nās* (most people), we know that something derogatory is about to be stated. On the other hand, when we see *ulu 'l-albāb* (those who have kernels) which means those who have centers, those whose hearts are awake, we can be sure that words of the highest praise are about to follow (see for example XIII, 19-24).

Every religion is concerned with the restoration of what was lost at the fall of man. For an ever increasing majority that cannot be achieved or even begun in this life. But there are bound to be a few who are capable of at least beginning the restoration now, and that is precisely why every religion possesses an inner aspect, the purpose of which is an immediate start of the task of regaining the direct consciousness of Transcendent Reality which the human soul lost at its fall. The Qur'ān expresses this loss in the words: *It is not the eyesights that are blind, but the hearts in the breasts that are blind* (XXIV, 46); and like all other esoterisms Sufism is initially concerned with what is often termed the opening of the Eye of the Heart.

Needless to say, however, the other four senses are no less direct than the faculty of sight, and the reader might be interested to know that for the revised and augmented edition of *Symbol and Archetype* about to be published by Fons Vitae, I have written an additional chapter on the symbolism of taste in connection with Ghazālī's definition of Sufism as *dhawq* (taste).

We have spoken of those who are on the right, that is, the saved. What of those on the left, the damned? Hell might seem to need some explanation because on the one hand the Quranic descriptions of the sufferings of Hell are unsurpassably terrible, yielding nothing in this respect to the Hindu, Buddhist and Christian descriptions of Hell, but on the other hand the Qur'ān insists that whereas every good deed is rewarded tenfold each sin is punished only with its equivalent (VI, 160). How then is it possible to deserve Hell? But before trying to answer this question we must first interrogate ourselves. We may think we are capable of assessing sinful acts such as murder or theft, and we hear not infrequently today of crimes so appalling and indicative of such a horrible state of soul that we might say no punishment but Hell is bad enough for this, until we remember that Hell is not just for a day or a week but seemingly endless. We will come back later to this question of duration; but are we capable of assessing the gravity of sins which are states lived without respite from one year's end to another like the sin of atheism to which we may add agnosticism? The Creator says in the Qur'ān: *I did not create jinn and men except that they should worship Me* (LI, 56). What makes man human is that he should reach beyond this world. The man who fails to worship is subhuman—and not merely that, as the Qur'ān points out, but even lower than the animals (XXV, 44). In short, man was created as representative of God on earth endowed with immense privileges such as no other earthly creature enjoys. In a very early Meccan revelation the Qur'ān affirms: *We created man in the fairest rectitude. Then cast We him down to be the lowest of the low, except for those who believe and who do the good deeds that piety demands* (XCV, 4-6).

The greatest of God's gifts to man at his creation is his power to conceive the Transcendent, nor does it begin in this life. The Qur'ān stresses that at the creation of Adam every human being later to be born into this world was imbued with the knowledge of the Divine Lordship. In other words every human being has in the depth of his nature a sense of the Absolute. According to the Qur'ān the sin of sins is turning one's back on the Transcendent in order to give all one's attention to this world, not as the representative of God but as a parody of God, a would-be independent tyrant out for an unrestrained and undirected exploitation of all the resources of the earthly state. This is the great betrayal of trust, and if Hell seems to have a touch of the Absolute it is because this betrayal is in relation to the Absolute. But Hell is not Absolute and cannot be Eternal for that is the prerogative of the Hidden Treasure alone. It is true that the Qur'ān speaks of the people of Hell as abiding therein forever, but this forever has to be understood in a relative sense, for there is one very explicit passage in which a double limitation is put on the everlastingness of Hell (XI, 103-108). Its inmates are described as abiding therein *so long as the heavens and the earth endure except as God wisheth. Verily God is ever the doer of what He will.* The first of the two limitations, *so long as the heavens and the earth endure*, can be interpreted "until the Creator reabsorbs the created universe back into Himself." As to the second limitation, it clearly refers to the possibility of a Divine intervention, and this is explained in a well known saying of the Prophet that after the Judgement, when the wretched are in Hell and the blessed are in Paradise, God will call together the Angels and the Prophets and the believers and bid them intercede for those in Hell, and in consequence a multitude of souls are released until finally He orders the release of all those in whom there is any good so that only those who have no good to their credit are left in Hell. Then He will say: "The Angels have interceded and the Prophets have interceded and the believers have interceded and none is left to intercede save the Most Merciful of the Merciful." And He will take out of Hell all who are left and will throw them into the River of Life at the entrance to the Gardens of Paradise.

The passage in the Qur'ān on which this is a commentary goes on to describe the blessed in Paradise as abiding therein so long as the heavens and the earth endure except as God wisheth. Apparently there is the same double limitation on the everlastingness of Paradise as on that of Hell, but this is not so, for Paradise, unlike Hell, is as it were open to the Absolute, in virtue of the highest Paradise, that of the Essence, which is the Absolute Itself. Thus in the Qur'ān immediately after what we have quoted there comes the reassuring promise in the definition of Paradise as a gift that shall not be taken away. The Prophet's explanation of this whole Quranic passage continues: "After the last people have been taken out of Hell God will turn to the people of Paradise and say: 'Are ye content?' And they will say: 'How should we not be content?' and He will say: 'I will give you better than this.' And they will say: 'What thing, O Lord, is better?' and He will say: 'I will enfold you in My Ridwān.'"

This is something which the highest Saints already know as we have seen. But the lower Paradises belong to the created universe which in the end also returns to the Creator *on the day when We shall roll up the heavens as at the rolling up of a written scroll* (XXI, 104). So Paradise is a gift that shall not be taken away because although in fact it is taken away it is replaced by the incomparably greater felicity of the Supreme Paradise which is no less than the Infinite and Eternal Beatitude of the Hidden Treasure from which all creation proceeds and to which it all returns.

In Christianity we can recall the words of Christ when he appeared to St. Juliana of Norwich who was greatly troubled by thoughts of the sufferings in Hell: "But all shall be well" to which, when he saw that she was not altogether satisfied he added: "All manner of thing[6] shall be well."

It could not be otherwise, for it must always be remembered that man is made in the image of God, and this means that it is not legitimate to attribute to Divine Providence anything that violates the God-given human sense of values, which includes the sense of responsibility. God knows that the worst sinners in Hell are totally innocent of one thing, namely their own existence, for which He alone is responsible. Thus the Qur'ān continually affirms that everything finally will be brought back to Him. In other words He is bound to reabsorb into the indescribable Felicity of His Own Essence everything which He manifested from it. *God's is the Sovereignty over the heavens and the earth; and unto God is the ultimate becoming* (XXIV, 42).

Notes

1. See René Guénon, *Fundamental Symbols*, 1995, p. 40. Now a Fons Vitae title. For lists of now available English translations of the books of Frithjof Schuon, René Guénon, Titus Burkhardt, and other spiritually informative writers, see Appendix 3 in the second edition of my book, *The Eleventh Hour* (Archetype, 2002).

2. On one occasion the Prophet is said to have likened ᶜAbū Bakr, the man who, as Caliph, succeeded him, to Abraham, and ᶜUmar, the second Caliph, to Moses. He is also said to have likened ᶜAli, the fourth Caliph, to Jesus.

3. See Martin Lings, *A Sufi Saint of the Twentieth Century*, London: Allen & Unwin, 1961, chapter XII: "A Spiritual Affinity."

4. *From the Divine to the Human*, Bloomington (Indiana): World Wisdom Books, 1981, p. 6.

5. The Sanskrit word *Māyā* means illusion as compared with *Ātmā* which expresses the Absolute Reality of the Divine Self. But *Māyā* is sometimes used in a positive sense to signify the Divine Art of Self-manifestation.

6. *Light on the Ancient Worlds*, London: Perennial Books, 1965, pp. 29-30.

7. *The Feathered Sun*, Bloomington (Indiana): World Wisdom Books, 1990, p. 70.

8. *From the Divine to the Human*, p. 97.

9. *Survey of Metaphysics and Esoterism*, Bloomington (Indiana): World Wisdom Books, pp. 71-72.

10. *Spiritual Perspectives and Human Facts*, London: Perennial Books, 1987, pp. 141–2.

11. I was privileged to be the disciple of my Shaykh for just over sixty years. A year or two before his death, he decided to appoint several successors to himself, one for each of the countries in which he had disciples. I was put in charge of the English *zāwiyah*; but not long after this, he wrote me a letter saying that he wanted me to take charge of his disciples in Morocco, Egypt, Jordan, the Indian Sub-

Continent, and Malaysia. To these he added the *zāwiyah* in Capetown which I had regularly been visiting on his behalf for more than twenty years. Our *ṭarīqah* in England, together with these prolongations, is now known as *aṭ-Ṭariqatu 'sh-Shādhiliyyatu 'd-Darqāwiyyatu 'LᶜAlawiyyatu 'l-Maryamiyyatu 's-Sirājiyyah.*

CHAPTER TWO

1. *The Eleventh Hour*, ch. 3; *Ancient Beliefs and Modern Superstitiions*, ch. 1.

2. *Summa Theologia.*

3. See Frithjof Schuon, *Islam and the Perennial Philosophy*, p. 36.

4. St. John, XVI: 12-15.

5. St. John, XV: 26.

6. See *Form and Substance in the Religions*, p.222.

CHAPTER THREE

1. St. Mark, XII, 30. In Deuteronomy VI, 5, to which this is a reference, the element "mind" is not mentioned, which makes no fundamental difference since the mind is strictly speaking a psychic faculty, and is therefore implicit in the word "soul." In St. Matthew, XXII, 37, on the other hand, the element "strength" is absent, which again makes no difference inasmuch as energy and endurance are dominated by the will, which is also a psychic faculty.

2. Ch. XIII (Harper and Row, 1975).

3. Martin Lings, *A Sufi Saint of the Twentieth Century*, p. 206.

4. William C. Chittick, *The Sufi Path of Knowledge*, p. 67.

5. As Frithjof Schuon has remarked, for those who come face to face with the founder of a new religion, the lack of alternative choice becomes as it were absolute in virtue of the correspondingly absolute greatness of the Divine Messenger himself. But with the passage of time there is inevitably a certain levelling out between the new and the less new, the more so in that the less new may have special claims on certain peoples.

6. "Aloof" and "introspective" are the epithets applied by Kenneth Cragg to the Eastern Churches, whom he severely criticizes in *The Call of the Minaret* for having done practically nothing throughout the centuries to convert the Islamic East to Christianity. It does not seem to occur to him that the qualities in question, though inconvenient for missionaries, are nearer to virtue than to vice. Moreover, the "aloofness" may well be in part a subconscious unwillingness to "rush in where angels fear to tread."

7. See p. 29.

8. For the ideal collective attitude of Judaism to Christianity, and for the reasons why it could never be realized, see Frithjof Schuon, *Islam and the Perennial Philosophy*, pp. 58-9.

9. This booklet, with the subtitle, *Guidelines for the Churches in their Relations with Muslim Communities* was published to coincide with the World of Islam Festival.

10. *First Apology*, Section 46. For the word "Reason", as translation of *logos*, we have substituted "Intellect."

11. *The Transcendent Unity of Religions* (Harper and Row, 1975), p.14.

12. *Ibid*, p. 20.

13. Muḥammad.

14. Muslims.

15. There is no general consensus of opinion as to what religion is referred to, and certain Muslim rulers, in India and elsewhere, have made the name in question a loophole for tolerance towards their non-Muslim, non-Christian and non-Jewish subjects.

16. An orthodox Jew, for example, deeply in love with the Hebrew Psalms, would be justified in hesitating to give up his religion for one that was based on a Revelation in a language he did not know; and he could use Quranic arguments to justify himself.

17. The verse we are considering is parallel to the words of Christ, "This Gospel of the Kingdom shall be preached in all the world. Then shall the end come", which likewise admit of both a limited and a universal interpretation, according to what is understood by "world." In its wider sense (as well as the narrower one) the first part of this prophecy has now come true inasmuch as every people on earth is now within easy reach of the gospel of the Kingdom, that is, the religion of Truth, in at least one of its modes.

18. That is, the great and lasting results which have been put to the test by centuries of time.

19. The answer of some Muslim theologians to this question has been, in all seriousness, that Almighty God has evidently decided to send the larger part of humanity astray, and that it is not for us to question His Wisdom. But faith on this basis can never be more than fragmentary. By such logic the mind surreptitiously robs itself of love, while turning a blind eye to some of the most essential Attributes of the Object of love. Another "explanation", shared also by Christians, *mutatis mutandis*, is that the "religion of Truth" (understood in a non-universal sense) will in fact prevail over the whole

world. *Veritas omnia vincit.* But if only one religion had been valid in the eyes of Heaven for the last thousand years or more, the expectation of a sudden total triumph of that true religion at the end of the cycle could not be enough to appease the mind, that is, it could not convincingly "exonerate" Providence from having allowed false religion to triumph so far and wide for so long.

20. *God doth what He will.* But it is clearly in the interests of man that a Divine intervention which founds a new religion should be overwhelmingly recognizable as such. The accompanying guarantees must be too tremendous, and too distinctive, to leave room for doubts in any but the most perverse, which means that certain kinds of things must be kept in reserve as the special prerogative of such a period. The Qur'ān refers to this "economy" when it affirms that questions which are put to God during the period of Revelation will be answered (V, 101), the implication being that after the Revelation has been completed, questions will no longer be answered so directly. It is as if a door between Heaven and earth were kept open during the mission of a Divine Messenger, to be closed at other times.

21. The change from first to third person with regard to the Divinity is frequent in the Qur'ān, and in fact, as we have already seen, I and He, at the highest level, are inseparable.

22. If He had sent only one religion to a world of widely differing affinities and aptitudes, it would not have been a fair test for all. He has therefore sent different religions, specially suited to the needs and characteristics of the different sectors of humanity.

CHAPTER FOUR

1. *Esoterism*, the chapter entitled "The Problem of Sexuality" (in the final edition pp. 129-145).

2. *Spiritual Perspectives and Human Facts*, Ghent (Sophia Perennis) 1969, p.29.

3. The reader might be interested to refer to my book *Splendours of Qur'ān Calligraphy and Illumination* (Thesaurus Islamicus Foundation), 2004.

4. St. Matthew, IV:18-19.

5. For the whole of the passage in question, see St John, XX: 24-29.

6. Ibn Ishaq, 886.

7. *Kitāb al-Maghāzi*, a chronicle of the Prophet's campaigns by Muḥammad ibn ᶜUmar al-Wāqidī, edited by Marsden Jones, p.725. For a more detailed account of the episode, see my biography of the Prophet, *Muḥammad: His Life Based on the earliest Sources*, pp.275-6.

8. The plural is used to include the guardian Angels.

9. For further details see my biography of the Prophet, *Muḥammad*, in the chapter entitled "After Khaybar" (the page and chapter numbers differ according to which edition it is).

CHAPTER FIVE

1. This Department has since then been transferred to The British Library.

2. This Centre, much expanded, is now the Regent's Park Mosque.

3. The Prophet said, "God will send to this community, at the head of every hundred years, one who will renew for it its religion."

4. *Sunan* (singular *sunnah*), that is, customs of the Prophet.

5. The Jews and the Christians.

6. *Dār al-Islām*, strictly speaking that part of the world that is under Islamic law, but here used more loosely to include any state that is officially Islamic.

CHAPTER SIX

1. Tirmidhī, XXXI, 79.

2. Muslim, LI, 4.

3. The order of the Surahs as they stand in the Qur'ān is not in the least chronological. The final order was presumably given to the Prophet by the Archangel after he had given him the final Revelation. Surah LVI, from which the immediately preceding quotations come, is a very early Meccan Revelation, whereas Surah L is considered to belong to the middle Meccan period.

4. See Chapter 3.

5. In particular al-Qashani. See Martin Lings, *The Book of Certainty*, which is largely based on this doctrine of the two Paradises.

6. In Anglo-Saxon some nouns retained their singular form for the plural and in St. Juliana's day this word was one of them. Today we still say "two or three sheep", for example.

IN MEMORIAM

Martin Lings on his ninety-sixth birthday, Kuala Lampur, Malaysia.

As Dr. Martin Lings passed into the Greater Life some thirty hours after completing this final work, we decided an *In Memoriam* might be of value. We thought that the many readers of Lings' works would appreciate a view of the author by Muslims and non-Muslims, those who simply met him, or heard him lecture, or those who received spiritual direction from him, and others who found sustenance from his writings. People have written to us from the world over and some of their tributes and recollections are included here to provide a more complete image of the man.

Whether people ever met him or not, they often referred to him as *Sidi Abu Bakr.* Abu Bakr was his traditional name given him on his conversion to Islam. Traditional names are taken in many religious traditions to distinguish between a person's secular and sacred life. The term *sidi* (*sayyida* for women) is used as a term of spiritual respect. The Japanese, similarly, add the syllable "-sen" to the name of a person being addressed which indicates respect for that person's "inner divinity." In the Eastern Orthodox Church—rather than say Mr. or Mrs.—"Your Godliness" might be used.

Still others refer to Martin Lings as *Shaykh* Abu Bakr, which indicates his role as a spiritual mentor or master. The word *shaykh* itself in Arabic literally means "elder" as does *geron* in Greek and *staretz* in Russian. In the traditional world, elders, as a whole, attain to wisdom, which is then imparted.

In some of the photographs included it will be noticed that traditional dress is worn, though usually only for prayer and devotion. One's garments act as a support to one's doing and state of being. Dr. Lings once mentioned that when an artist of the Middle Ages wished to paint an angel, he simply attired the angel in the flowing clothes of the day. One could hardly paint an angel, he said, in most modern clothing but could do so in the daily garments worn in such places as North Africa, Pakistan, and India. In his words, *After the body, the clothes are the next nearest environment to the human soul and have an incalculable effect upon it, as the ancients well knew… To have an objective view of the anti-spiritual nature of modern fashions, it is enough to remember that in the sacred art of many civilizations blessed Spirits in Paradise are pictorially represented, without the least incongruity, in clothes that were worn by the artist and his contemporaries. …*

The Publisher

Shaykh Abū Bakr Sirāj ad-Dīn
at Sultan Hasan Mosque, Cairo, Egypt.

The Departure of Shaykh Abu Bakr Siraj al-Din
By His Excellency The Grand Mufti of Egypt, Shaykh Dr. Ali Gomaa

A great man departed from this world Thursday morning the 12th of May. He passed away at his home in Kent, England, and was buried at his home in the garden which he raised and cared for out of his love for flowers and beauty. Shaykh Martin Lings, who adopted the name Abu Bakr Siraj al-Din, was born in Lancashire, January, 1909, to a Protestant family. His parents loved him dearly and perceived in him intelligence, even sainthood, from an early age so that they never opposed him in anything, not even when God blessed him with Islam.

He spent some of his early childhood in America where his father worked, and upon returning to England, began his formal education at Clifton College where his skills as a leader first became apparent. In 1928 he entered Oxford University where he read English Literature under C.S. Lewis who found in him not only an insightful student but also a friend and companion. After his graduation Lings taught English Literature in Lithuania.

Lings had two friends who shared his inquisitive spirit which led him on his search for Truth. One of them, Patterson, became a Muslim, took on the name Sidi Hussein Nur al-Din, and is buried in the Mamluk cemetery in Cairo. The other friend found Islam in a different way and took on the name Sidi Daud; he died in England. Patterson had traveled to China seeking truth in Confucianism while Lings, having been unable to find what he sought in his conversion to Catholicism, decided to travel to India to study Hinduism. During his journey, Lings encountered the French Muslim intellectual René Guénon in Cairo in 1940. Guénon, who had taken on the name Shaykh Abd al-Wahid Yahya, passed away in 1950 and is buried in Cairo near Lings' friend Hussein. Guénon's children continue to live in Cairo to this day, may God bless them. In Guénon, Lings found what he had been searching for. He had earlier converted to Islam and when Patterson returned to Cairo, he converted as well. He, too, taught in Cairo University, then called Fuad the First, and he later died in a horse-riding accident.

In 1944 Lings married Lesley Smalley who also embraced Islam, taking the name Rabia. She continues to live in their home in Kent after the passing of her lifelong partner whose intellectual vision she shared for over sixty years.

Lings lived in Cairo near the pyramids in the village of Nazlat al-Saman until 1952. The traditional Egyptian garments he always wore were cut by Hajj Ashour, a saintly person among the Friends of God, may God have mercy on them all, whose shop was at the entrance of the Khan al-Khalili. Lings would have loved to spend the rest of his life in Egypt had it not been for political interference. There were demonstrations against the British after the 1952 revolution, three of his colleagues were killed, and British professors at the University were dismissed.

Returning to London at that stage of life made it a difficult homecoming. The competition in academia required more than having held teaching positions in Lithuania and Egypt, so it became necessary for him to acquire a PhD. It was at this time that *The Book of Certainty*, which he had written in Arabic while in Egypt as *Kitab al-Yaqīn al-Madhhab al-Sūfī fī'l-Imān*, was published. He got a bachelor's degree in Arabic followed by a PhD for which he wrote a dissertation on Shaykh Ahmad al-Alawi which was subsequently published under the title *A Sufi Saint of the Twentieth Century*. This turned out to be one of his most influential books representing as it did a unique vision of Islamic spirituality from within. In 1955 he assumed a post at the British Museum where he began to focus on Quranic calligraphy. His book, *The Art of Quranic Calligraphy and Illumination*, was published by The World of Islam Festival in 1976 to coincide with that celebration in London.

Lings spent the next thirty years writing for his increasing readership and following. Among his writings are: *Muhammad: his life based on the earliest sources* published in 1973, and *Shakespeare in the Light of Sacred Art* published in 1966 and reissued in 1984 with an introduction by H.R.H. The Prince of Wales under the title *The Secret of Shakespeare* in which he examines the spiritual roots and symbolism of Shakespeare's writings. A new and expanded edition will be published in 2006. His book, *The Art of Quranic Calligraphy and Illumination*, was reissued in a new edition in 2004 under the title *Splendours of Quran Calligraphy and Illumination*. His work, *Mecca*, was recently published in 2004, and it is now followed by *A Return to the Spirit* published posthumously.

Lings' encounter with René Guénon had a considerable effect on him, resulting in the expansion of an enlightened guidance of what came to be known as the Traditionalist School (*Madrasat al-Turāth*), in which the materialism of the modern world was criticized and contrasted with the wisdom present in the heart of all revealed religions, whether Hinduism, Buddhism, Judaism, Christianity, or Islam. This wisdom is the essential light (*fitrah*) God created in the hearts of all men by which they can be brought to the Truth. (Read Sura Rūm, v.20.) Lings lived in the light of that guidance until the end of his blessed life.

Martin Lings came to Islam through the Swiss Shaykh, 'Isa Nur-al-Dīn. Shaykh 'Isa himself had converted by way of the great Algerian saint Ahmad al-'Alawi whose *tarīqa* remains active to this day in Mostaghānem, Algeria, and whose books are published and widespread.

Lings had a deep interest in the symbolism of colors, their delineation and development among the Muslims. He writes in his *Splendours of Quran Calligraphy and Illumination*:

> Colour is used towards the same ends as form. Gold was the initial element; and after a short period of fluctuation, that is, by the middle of the fourth/tenth century, blue had been given a marked precedence over both green and red, and it was soon raised to the level of parity with gold in the East, whereas in the West gold retained its original supremacy with blue as second.
>
> If blue liberates by Infinitude, gold liberates because, like the sun, it is a symbol of the Spirit and therefore virtually transcends the whole world of forms. Gold, by its very

nature, "escapes" from form to the point that a calligrapher writing in gold has to outline his letter with black in order to make them formally effective. As the colour of light, gold is, like yellow, intrinsically a symbol of knowledge. Extrinsically, it means teaching or manifestation. Blue in the presence of gold is therefore Mercy inclined to reveal itself.

We have mentioned here a small portion of Lings' contribution, which was, and will remain, of great significance to a world sunk in confusion. It was, however, his personality that so deeply affected those who knew him, especially the large number of young people who sought him out for spiritual advice. This will remain with them for the rest of their lives in the fear that they will never meet the likes of him again. May God have Mercy on him, and bless us with more of his kind.

We need to study these great people who have converted to Islam in a manner that confirms the universality of this religion and its appropriateness for all times and places.

> Translated from the *Al-Ahram International Edition*,
> June 11, 2005, by Nuri Friedlander (Cairo, Egypt)
> and Jean-Louis Michon (Geneva, Switzerland).

Thou Hast Departed

How sad to hear that thou hast departed,
Leaving this lowly world for the luminous beyond.
Thy gentle voice, uttering words of wisdom slowly.
Deliberately like honey being gently poured,
Not to be heard again in this transient realm.
Nor thy writings new to be beheld by eager eyes,
Accustomed to the outpouring of pearls of wisdom,
From thy gracious pen for decades on end.

How in days of old we circumambulated the Ka'bah.
And wandered amidst the turquoise blue mosques of Isfahan.
How we paid homage to the saints of Marrakesh,
Walking in remembrance to those sacred sites away hidden.
How oft we visited holy places in Cairo and celebrated
        His Glory,
On continents stretching from East to West.
These joyous moments are to be no more here below,
How sad then to hear that thou hast departed.

And yet joyous it is indeed to recall thy long life,
A life so rich, bearing so much spiritual fruit,
That has nourished souls from near and far.
Thou hast departed but thy words and memories remain,
Etched on the tablet of our hearts, on the substance of our souls.
Dear friend of God, may the doors of His Grace upon thee open.
May we again by the Kawthar* meet, if He wills.
There to contemplate in harmony the infinite Beauty,
The dazzling Splendor of the Face of the Friend.

Seyyed Hossein Nasr
Washington, D.C.

Written a day after the death of Shaykh Abū Bakr Sirāj al-Dīn al-Shādhilī, al-Darqāwī, al-'Alawī, al-Maryamī—*raḍī Allāhu 'anhu*—to whom this poem is dedicated.

*A river of Paradise according to the Quran.

EXCERPTS FROM *THE INDEPENDENT*
LONDON, MAY 21, 2005

MARTIN LINGS

ISLAMIC SCHOLAR AND MASTER OF SUFISM

… Martin Lings was one of the most eloquent and serene Western voices in the Islamic world. Through his rich and varied oeuvre, translated into more than a dozen languages, Lings transmitted a certain vision of the sacred as embodied in Sufism, the esoteric, spiritual dimension of Islam.

He combined vast knowledge with meticulous scholarship, a poetic sensibility and an elegant expression, which made the most profound subjects accessible, and enthralled the large audiences who flocked to his lectures. His intellectual power was tempered with the gentleness and the humility of the Sufi, and in old age he had acquired the aura of one who had striven all his life towards sanctity. …

At the time when so much nonsense is talked about "the clashes of civilizations" and Islam is under siege, the work of Martin Lings shines like a beacon. He lived in a modest cottage in the middle of woods in Kent. A keen and original gardener, he created a small but ravishing garden with a view over the undulating country all around. He was laid to rest among the flowers and plants he had lovingly cultivated.

Shusha Guppy

EXCERPTS FROM *THE GUARDIAN*
LONDON, MAY 27, 2005

MARTIN LINGS

ISLAMIC SCHOLAR CONCERNED WITH SPIRITUAL CRISIS

In spite of his great age the death of Martin Lings (Shaykh Abu Bakr Siraj ad-Din) on the morning of May 12th came as a shock to his many friends and, in particular, to those who had regularly sought his spiritual counsel over the years. Only ten days previously he had addressed an audience of 3,000 at the Wembley Conference Centre on the occasion of the Prophet Muhammad's birthday. Earlier this year, at the time of his 96th birthday, he had traveled to Egypt, Dubai, Pakistan, and Malaysia, still vigorous. It was all too easy for his friends to believe that he might be immune to the frailties which afflict lesser men and, insofar as he remained serene, tolerant, and endlessly patient to the end, this was true. ...

Charles Le Gai Eaton

EXCERPTS FROM *THE NEW YORK TIMES*
NEW YORK, MAY 29, 2005

MARTIN LINGS, A SUFI WRITER ON ISLAMIC IDEAS,
DIES AT 96

Martin Lings, a widely acclaimed British scholar whose books on Islamic philosophy, mysticism and art reflected his own deep belief in Sufism, the esoteric, purely spiritual dimension of Islam, died on May 12 at his home in Westerham, Kent County, England. He was 96. ...

His own personal intellectual and spiritual journey reflected his friendship with the philosophers René Guénon and Frithjof Schuon, who saw modern history as a sorry record of decline, and man's salvation in traditional religion. Dr. Lings followed them in converting to Sufi Islam, about which he wrote the entry in the *Encyclopaedia Britannica*.

He was considered by some, including initiates he instructed, to be a Sufi saint, and by many non-Muslims to be a provocative intellectual.

In the foreword to Dr. Lings' *The Sacred Art of Shakespeare: To Take Upon Us the Mystery of Things*, Prince Charles wrote, "Lings' particular genius lies in his ability to convey, as perhaps no one else has ever done, the theatrical underpinnings of these texts, leaving readers with deep and lasting impressions not only of those masterpieces of dramatic artistry, but of the extraordinary man behind them as well." ...

Douglas Martin

Each of us is called one day to leave this world. One of the hadiths of the Prophet Muhammad tells us that only three things remain from a human being's earthly passage: useful knowledge transmitted to others, charitable works dedicated to the poor, and finally, a pious child who prays for its parents. From these three elements, I note the first as the legacy left by Abu Bakr, Martin Lings.

In effect, from my own personal knowledge, as well as the numerous testimonies of our brothers and sisters, this man, nourished many souls in their quest for Truth through his writings, especially those about the life of the Prophet Muhammad and other works dealing with Sufism and the Islamic tradition.

Through his celebrated book, *A Sufi Saint of the 20th Century: Sheikh al-Alawi*, he especially contributed to enhanced knowledge of this exceptional spiritual master, by spreading the writings of a man who was a revitalizer of the Sufi tradition and who indelibly marked the 20th Century by his presence, his action, and his efforts to bring East and West closer together.

It is with great respect that we give homage today to Abu Bakr, Martin Lings, through his works, and we pray for the peace of his soul.

> Shaykh Khaled Bentounes
> Shadhlia Darkawiya Alawiya Community
> (Spiritual great-grandson of Shaykh al Alawi)

IN MEMORIAM

It is with deep personal sadness that I learned of the passing of Martin Lings. He was an extraordinary man and an inspiration to us all; his passing represents the end of an era.

The depth and breadth of his knowledge of the Islamic world remains unsurpassed and he will be sadly missed by all who came to know him. He will be missed also for his tireless work to deepen the understanding of the Islamic faith and Islamic spirituality. Through his writings and example he helped others find that inner liberation which can effect change in the world for the good of humankind.

His personal spirituality, respect for human dignity and patience infused all he did, and was an example to all who came into contact with him. How apt that he should have addressed an audience of some 3,000 people only ten days before he died. I am sure that none will have left his talk untouched by the quiet energy and encouragement of his words.

El Hassan bin Talal
Royal Palace
Amman, Jordan

In Memoriam

I first met Shaykh Abu Bakr at a lecture he gave in Magdalen College, Oxford on the "Quranic Doctrine of the Afterlife and Sufism." I had seen his name on a book once but knew very little either about the topic or about the speaker. Entering the small room adjacent to the College Chapel, I laid eyes for the first time on the venerable, silver-haired figure sitting at the head of the table who was about to transform my life. As he began to speak, almost like a flash of lightning, I realized that, for the first time in my life, I was in the presence of a perfected soul—something I had barely ever conceived of, let alone encountered. He spoke as only one who has a direct vision of the Truth can. An otherworldly light seemed to shine from his face, so radiantly that I could not maintain my gaze at him without turning away every few moments. I was gripped by the certainty that this was what a saint was, and what it meant to be True Man—a certainty that has never left me.

We send you, *Mawlana*, our most profound gratitude and love, and look forward to the reunion in the Hereafter.

KN
London, England

95

In short, Shaykh Abu Bakr Siraj al-Din (Martin Lings) was a sort of paradigm of the essence of that timeless spirituality that is commonly shared by practicing adherents of all truly monotheistic faiths, with a special emphasis on the virtues of a limitless compassion and understanding. He was also a profound Islamic scholar and great lover of the universal message of its Prophet (peace be upon him) who brought his knowledge of classical learning, eastern and western, to its service, greatly assisting the much-needed effort in modern times to provide explanations and answers to spiritual questions involving "how" and "why" with deeply reasoned guidance, whenever sought. In addition, he was as sensitive to the beauties of manuscripts, arts, and crafts and their inherent as well as symbolic meaning, as he was to the delicate vagaries of human nature, well able to put into suitable rich language all that he comprehended and beheld and wanted to express and portray. The world of Islam has indeed lost in him a great, great scholar and mentor. May the Almighty rest his soul in eternal peace and keep his wife in his benign care and sound health. Ameen.

> From the Family of
> Sultan Ghalib Al-Qu'aiti
> Jeddah, Kingdom of Saudi Arabia

TEARS AT A WEDDING: A LETTER OF CONDOLENCE TO FRIENDS OF MARTIN LINGS

As we know, in Pakistan the *mulid* of a saint, celebrated on the anniversary of his/her death, is called the "*urs:*" the wedding celebration. It commemorates when the saint was brought into union with the Beloved. Weddings are joyful celebrations.

Yet those who knew the saint must give up his/her earthly companionship for at least awhile, or so it seems to them. They may not see him or touch him; they feel the pain of separation. They may weep; it is permitted.

It is much like the tears that we shed at the wedding of beloved children. We are happy, but the transition produces tears; not just tears of joy, in resonating souls, but tears of awe. We know they have set their feet within a great *mysterion*, (*sirr* in

Arabic): one where we cannot accompany them. Of course, in the Greek Church, *mysterion* or mystery is also the word used for what the Western Church calls a sacrament.

But we are much blest; because of the great mystery that the Christian creed calls "the communion of the saints." They are available to us in Reality (*al-Haqq*); they help us, and even sometimes appear to us or speak to us. Death is truly swallowed up in the Light that is our Life. Alleluia!

Professor John Williams
College of William and Mary
Williamsburg, Virginia

SAD NEWS—THE PASSING ON OF MARTIN LINGS

Verily from Allah we come and to Him we return.
I received today from a former student the news of the passing of the Sufi leader and scholar Martin Lings/Abu Bakr Siraj al-Din. He was in his nineties, I believe. His recent bilingual edition of Arabic Sufi poetry (*Sufi Poems: A mediaeval Anthology*) showed that he had not lost at all his rare talent for translating with accuracy in an elegant classical style.

Here's a sample of Lings' translation in this anthology (verse attributed to Abu'l-Hosayn Nuri):

> From time I'm veiled; my veil is my concern for Him, My wonder at His infinite worth transcending mine. That I am absent from its grasp time see-eth not, And I perceive not time's events how they flow on, Since I am all attendance to fulfill His due, Nor care I, all of my life long, for the hand of time.

Our grandfather in Islam, Martin Lings, has traveled to meet his Creator in the eternity of the next life.

May Allah forgive him and grant him a high place in paradise. Verily, we shall meet again soon. *Al-Fātiḥa.*

Jawid Mojaddedi
Department of Religion,
Rutgers
New Brunswick, New Jersey

Epitaph for Martin Lings

Sidi Abu Bakr Siraj al-Din has folded his tent.
In him was manifest the seamless union of true Islam,
    true universality, and true sanctity.
As he bore the burden of Paradise for his
    companions in this world,
So may his companions in the Garden now return
    him that favor.

His vessel was unbroken.

> Charles Upton
> Lexington, Kentucky

The Passing of the Shaykh

When the great ones die
    there's a sound in the world that
      sounds like angel song ...

With prayers on our beloved Prophet Muhammad, and his Companions and all the *awliyya* (saints), my greeting and embrace, *Ma-salaama*.

> Daniel Abdal-Hayy Moore
> Philadelphia, Pennsylvania

A REFLECTION

Dr. Lings—for those of us who had tender affection and high regard for him—was a man who was what he knew and loved. When encountering him, one knew that one was in the presence of a truly spiritual light. I have never met a person who so deeply and sublimely manifested the Spirit, so much so that one could see little of a "personality," but rather one saw someone who had so done away with the ego that the divine qualities, the *asma' Allah*, were communicated clearly through his modest being. His greatness was precisely in his humility.

Ann Birkelbach
Arlington, Virginia

IN MEMORIAM: MARTIN LINGS

I never met Martin Lings but several times over the years we spoke on the phone. Every time, it happened that he had just come in from the garden; and each time it was remarkable how the smell of the flowers and the smell of the earth came through the telephone line with more power than the sound of any words.

Peter Kingsley
Author of *Reality* and *In the Dark Places of Wisdom*
Point Richmond, California

OUR FRIEND

Of those from whom I have learned wisdom and truth, Martin Lings occupies a special niche of serene and gracious spirituality, a heavenly light on the Path.

My husband and I treasure the memory of our visit with Dr. Lings at his home in Kent. He himself opened his front door to welcome us. We remember most his humble smile and soft voice and the kindness he showed us, and the time he gave us. Many other of his kindnesses over the years are precious memories.

By word, books, letters and example Martin Lings graced my life. His gentle and wise presence stays with me as my prayers for him ascend.

In deepest gratitude,
Louise Wilson,
Vancouver Island, British Columbia

Sidi Abu Bakr

Martin Lings is the first person whom I have met for whom the thought arose, "I would like to be like that." There have been many others, whom I have met, with wonderful qualities that I would gratefully emulate if possible. But I had never had a feeling like this before. The gratitude for this cannot be expressed.

The presence with him was so radiant, beautiful, loving, and, above all, transcendent and unbounded. I do not otherwise, at this time, know very much about him, his life, works, or writings. But that does not seem to matter. I have known more about others, but not this Thinking about him, only the little Upanishadic (*chhandogya*) verse keeps coming to mind: *Tat tvam asi* ... That thou art.

Carol Weingarten
Tryon, North Carolina

Reflection on Shaykh Abu Bakr

When I first met Shaykh Abu Bakr, I knew at once and beyond a doubt that I had met a "worthy man." Sri Nisargadatta had taught me what to look for: "When you meet a worthy man," he said, "you will love and trust him and follow his advice. This is the role of the realized people—to set an example of perfection for others to admire and love. Beauty of life and character is a tremendous contribution to the common good."

From the moment Shaykh Abu Bakr greeted us at his small front door and helped us across his threshold, I saw what we can become. As he took my hand in his and helped us into his place of prayer and meditation, I knew the living example. When he spoke to us of his life and about spiritual matters, his essence overwhelmed his words: what was said and shared and given shone brightly but somehow the beauty of his being illuminated more. When we departed, I could only think: "Today God has truly shown me one of His own. Through this man and the Grace of God, I have seen what God asks of us and how far we can go towards Him."

This inspiration stays with me. It seems a vast and important "contribution to the common good," a gift of Love freely given to those who remember him and remain.

> Richard Weingarten
> Tryon, North Carolina

On His Passing

> The first rose's bloom
> Is now gone, but uncovers,
> Beneath, many buds!

> Salim Abd al-Hayy
> Indiana

He was truly effulgent. There was nothing pretentious about his demeanor. I heard him at a lunchtime Islamic seminar here in London during my first year in the fall of '97. His tranquility and *gravitas* left one wondering whether he was touched by Gabriel's wing.

> A student from India

Between 1964 and 1966, I was studying ancient manuscripts in Martin Lings' office in the British Museum's Oriental Reading Room. On one occasion, I asked him what he liked about Cairo, which he often visited. "The graveyards," he replied. When he learned why I was studying old calligraphic works, he said I could never learn calligraphy well, or if I did, the Arabs would never accept me. In this he was right, more or less.

May God have mercy on his gentle soul, and upon us.

> Mohamed Zakariya
> Arlington, Virginia

101

ABOUT MARTIN LINGS

Four peonies float from a vase, vertically, and their petals are light pink, the centers, yellow-gold, with red velvet bee portals. As this vision of beauty pervades the cold, nighttime room, I think of Martin Lings, able to enter there at the doorway of the Spring flowers, to peace, love, beauty. The entry is symmetrical. Petals drape themselves in unearthly hangings, beyond our ability to duplicate them. They are wondrous. Didn't he know we are seeing ourselves, that we belong to the One, that our dance is costumed in these soft, brief blooms? His influence travels with me, as I take his writings along. I am most grateful for his existence here.

Nana Lampton
Goshen, Kentucky

STORIES OF DR. LINGS

In the late 1990s, I once had an interview with him in which I spoke of several troubling problems. After I rattled off a list of these "problems," Shaykh Abu Bakr paused and finally gave the following response (I paraphrase since I did not record it word-for-word): "The *Tarīqah* is like a grand, magnificently beautiful cathedral. These problems you mention are like irregularities in one sole block of this huge cathedral; instead of noting the grandeur and beauty of the cathedral, you are focusing on the irregularities of this one block ...."

Ever since, whenever I find myself troubled by such things, I recall those wise words, which reduce the "problems" practically to nothing.

Mark Bonadio
Bloomington, Indiana

GOLD AND BLUE

Gold and blue are two colours that Dr Martin Lings loved and which his publishers despaired over. He very often asked for these difficult-to- reproduce colours on the covers of his books; he could see in them subtle shades that were invisible to our eyes, and it is no wonder that this is the case, for these colours were very close to his own luminous and celestial soul.

Having worked closely with him on the last book he published with the Islamic Texts Society, *Sufi Poems: A Mediaeval Anthology*, we would like to include a poem he selected and translated from Ghazālī as a tribute to him, the like of whom we shall never see again, *raḍiya Allāh ʿanhu wa-qaddasa sirrah.*

> Say unto my brethren when they see me dead,
> And weep for me, lamenting me in sadness:
> "Think ye I am this corpse ye are to bury?
> I swear by God, this dead one is not I.
> I in the Spirit am, and this my body
> My dwelling was, my garment for a time.
> I am a treasure: hidden I was beneath
> This talisman of dust, wherein I suffered.
> I am a pearl; this shell imprisoned me,
> But leaving it, all trials I have left.
> I am a bird, and this was once my cage;
> But I have flown, leaving it as a token.
> I praise God who hath set me free, and made
> For me a dwelling in the heavenly heights.
> Ere now I was a dead man in your midst,
> But I have come to life, and doffed my shroud."

al-Fātiḥa

Fatima Azzam
Islamic Texts Society
Cambridge, United Kingdom

In Memoriam

Each year for almost the last 20 years Dr. Martin Lings graced the shores of Cape Town with a two-week sojourn. We met for the last time in February 2005. Dr Lings and his wife who accompanied him on all his visits, was staying in a small rustic cottage overlooking a valley reaching out to the Atlantic Ocean. During his stay he would have regular dinners with small groups of friends, attend *majalis* and go for brisk and lengthy walks with friends along the slopes of the Table Mountain range. These walks were deeply personal and spiritually enriching occasions where Dr Lings would devote his time to address questions raised by friends. During these precious times we basked in the depth and breadth of his profound wisdom. It was his spiritual knowledge, the radiance of his presence, the graciousness of his being and his gentleness of expression, which drew us all ever closer to him. The changes he made in our lives were deep and lasting. These memorable meetings will forever be embedded in our hearts and minds. A great scholar and noble Muslim has departed from this world. May Allah grant him a special place in *Jannah*, *Insha-Allah*.

Yusuf ibn Muhammad
Cape Town, South Africa

Two Certainties

To try and describe in few words the personality of Martin Lings, Shaykh Abu Bakr, now that he has left this world, seems to be an impossible task, so filled with fine features and qualities was his physical as well as his moral and spiritual nature, and so dedicated was he to fulfill a number of varied, useful and delicate tasks. I will then limit myself to share with those who feel concerned by the departure of this noble servant and friend of God two certainties which have been constantly on my mind, and several times on my lips, since he passed away.

The first certainty imposed itself upon me just after "the sad news" had arrived on the telephone, as soon as the shock and sobs of the intense grief had subsided. It brought with it a serenity which accompanied me during the next day—May 13, 2005—spent in the house and flowering garden of the deceased, a serenity which lit up the faces wet with tears, of his dear and respected wife and of the many close friends attending the funeral. I had then realized that a man so fundamentally pure as Martin Lings could never have committed a serious sin; during all his life; and I felt sure that he was henceforth blessed with the highest favors promised in Paradise to those who have never deviated from the righteous Way.

As for the second certainty, it has to do with what Shaykh Abu Bakr has completed in his life and has left for the present and the future seekers of Truth. It is sufficient to evoke the scruple, the patience and the intensity with which he practiced and taught the universal ideals of devotion to the One God and of love for the neighbor, this during the long span of life that was granted to him, to measure the scope of his influence on three generations of seekers of Truth and Beauty. What he leaves behind him in terms of oral advice to travelers on the mystic path, of written works and testimonies on symbolism, on Sufism, on the lives of Prophet Muhammad and Shaykh Ahmad al-'Alawī, makes us think that every part and parcel of this heritage may bring fruits. This gives to his mission an indestructible value and to his presence among us a touch of eternity.

Jean-Louis Michon
Genève, Switzerland

SHAYKH ABU BAKR

In his pamphlet *Proofs of Islam*, Shaykh Abu Bakr writes that the Prophet Muhammad's presence gave man a "Taste of the Infinite and the Eternal"; it is not too much to say that Shaykh Abu Bakr's own presence, through the purity, wisdom and sweetness of his soul, and the boundless love that he bestowed upon his many followers across the world, also gave us a "Taste of the Infinite and the Eternal"; to know him was to love him.

> Emma Clark
> The Prince of Wales Foundation
> London, United Kingdom

INNĀ LIᶜLLĀHI WA INNĀ ILAIHI RĀJIŪN
(WE BELONG TO HIM AND TO HIM WE RETURN).

The news of the Islamic scholar, respected Martin Lings' death is quite saddening to us all. But a lover of the Prophet, a person who lived a spiritually fulfilling life will meet his Lord with rewards and honor. We are the ones who will be deprived of his contributions and inspiration.

May Allah open the doors of *Jannah* (Paradise) for him and cover him with His mercy. We will remember him for his contribution to the understanding of Islam and building bridges of understanding.

> Sayyid M. Syeed, Ph.D.
> Secretary General
> Islamic Society of North America
> Plainfield, Indiana

106

A Tribute to a Great and Loving Soul

Although I never met Dr. Lings, his letters saved me. In 1995, I made a decision to embrace Islam. This decision had been preceded by a number of years of questioning of certain aspects of Christianity, questions which had been prompted initially by living among Muslims and experiencing the solidity of their convictions, as well as other influences, both intellectual and emotional. For a number of years, however, Christianity has been the rockbed of my life, and Christ utterly central and beloved. (The fact is that he remains so to this day, about which I will have more to say in what follows). In reality, my conversion to Islam (or, as I prefer to call it, my semi-conversion) was influenced powerfully by a desire for a sense of acceptance and belonging, and was only partially a result of solid conviction. As a result, the step I had taken soon led to a dark night of the soul, the depths of which were destined to transform me forever, and in ways I never could have anticipated. Within a couple of weeks of my decision to profess Islam, I began waking up in the middle of the night in a cold sweat, thinking of Jesus' words that whoever denies him before men, He will deny before his Heavenly Father. I was, in a nearly literal sense, beside myself: in a labyrinth in which, whichever way I turned, more unanswered, and seemingly unanswerable, questions arose. As I immersed myself in writings by Christians in proof of Christianity and disproof of Islam, as well as writings by Muslims in proof of Islam and disproof of Christianity, my confusion and anxiety only intensified until they nearly led me to the breaking point. On one side there was the abyss into which, according to my understanding of Christian teachings, I'd plunge myself by remaining in Islam and, on the other side, the abyss into which, according to my understanding of Muslim teachings, I would plunge myself by reaffirming a Christian profession. It was hell on earth. Desperate and paralyzed, I was being pulled limb from limb on a spiritual "rack." I had plunged myself into spiritual and emotional chaos by entering what appeared to be a formidable, monolithic, uncompromising religious system which challenged the core premises of my "home faith" without having been fully convinced beforehand, and I was on the brink of madness. The more I read, the more the claims of the two faiths seemed to balance out into a terrifying sort of deadlock, since both were claiming to be "*the* way of salvation." On one side I had dear Christian friends telling me that I was "intellectualizing," while my closest Muslim friends would tell me that my leanings toward Christian teaching were "invalid" since they didn't work out intellectually (as they saw it). With Christians praying for me to remain/become a Christian and Muslims praying for me to remain/become a Muslim, I felt like a walking battleground.

Something that struck me repeatedly in the course of this ordeal is how both Christianity and Islam include a distinct emphasis on (a) the hereafter, and (b) hellfire for those who turn away from their respective messages. And I found myself wondering: Is it just possible that, in light of the difficulty— nay, impossibility—I face when I contemplate rejecting *either one* definitively in favor of the other, that such dire warnings of hellfire, damnation, and so forth have been placed in both messages not so much because God's Truth is to not be found anywhere else or in any other form, but for the sake of our dichotomy-bound minds, our need for order in the midst of a universe which, if we could penetrate further into its mysteries, would overwhelm us with its very non-dichotomousness?

During those tumultuous days, I wrote to Dr. Lings with some of my questions and doubts connected with Islam, and he, despite his busy schedule and the many demands on him, wrote me back in longhand, responding to my questions one by one. In the context of the other things he said, he quoted Qur'an 5:48 in which God declares, *Unto every one of you have We appointed a [different] law and way of life. And if God had so willed, He could surely have made you all one single community: but He willed it otherwise in order to test you by means of what He has vouchsafed unto you.* In point of fact, it was this one verse, more than any other point he made in either of his letters to me, that ministered most to my need. And minister it did.

The intensity and depth of the suffering I had already gone through by the time I wrote to Dr. Lings had alienated me for all time from an insistence on seeing Truth in black-and-white terms (at least, Truth as perceived "in a glass darkly" here in this vale of tears). No, I said: If things remain that unclear, and unbearably confusing, after being presented with all the "facts" from both sides, there has to be something fundamentally flawed about the exclusive, absolutist, black/white, either/or way of looking at things. In short, God simply has to be more all-encompassing and merciful than that. This verse which Dr. Lings quoted from the Qur'an confirmed, and helped me to embrace, this growing conviction of mine.

In his wonderful book, *A Sufi Saint of the Twentieth Century: Shaikh Ahmad Al-'Alawi*, Dr. Lings contrasts Islam as a "way of knowledge" with Christianity as a "way of love," which admits of less interest in other religions than Islam does. And in this context he observes:

> The full Islamic perspective, that is, the Qur'anic perspective, is far too vast for the average Moslem. The words, *For each of you We have appointed a law and traced out a path, and if God had so willed, He would have made you one community* (Qur'an 5:48) remain for him little more than a dead letter, and the same may be said of many other verses such as, *For every community there is a messenger* (Qur'an 10:47), and *Verily, We have sent messengers before thee. About some We have told thee, and about some have We not told thee*, and *Verily, the faithful, and the Jews and the Sabians and the Christians—whoso believeth in God and the Last Day and doeth deeds of piety—no fear shall come upon them, neither shall they grieve* (5:69).

For me, though, these are far from a dead letter. On the contrary, they are cause for rejoicing, a balm to my soul, and a reason for the love that I came to have for Sidi Abu Bakr, sight unseen.

When I've gone back to church and listened to the gospel reading, I've had an overwhelmingly intense feeling of "homecoming" and solace. When I listen to the reading, it feels as though it's "mine," directed to me in a way which I may not have experienced if I hadn't been away for so long, feeling as though I'd "locked myself out" and couldn't come back.

Hence, I speak sometimes of my Christian "sympathies," a term which I hope helps to convey this heart-experience of homecoming, belonging and, indeed, faith, yet without it being a clear, down-the-line acceptance of every single formulated Christian doctrine. After all I've been through, the boundaries of "truth vs. untruth" on an earthly level will never again be crisp the way they once appeared to me. As Peter once said, *Truly I perceive that God shows no partiality, but in every nation any one who fears him and does what is right is acceptable to him* (Acts 10:34). And as the Qur'an declares forthrightly, *Verily, those who have attained to faith [in this divine writ], as well as those who follow the Jewish faith, and the Christians, and the Sabians—all who believe in God and the Last Day and do righteous deeds—shall have their reward with their Sustainer; and no fear shall they have, and neither shall they grieve* (2:62).

The Oxford History of Christianity concludes with a chapter entitled, "The Future of Christianity" by John Taylor in which the author makes what to me is a fascinating, deeply consoling statement. He says,

> Religious pluralism will certainly be a significant fact of life in the next century and a new quality of relationship among the major religions is bound to develop. *Instead of seeing one another as rivals... they are likely to become more aware of the rise of irreligion and spiritual indifference in the world, and may see themselves as fellow witnesses to the reality of God.* [italics mine] (p. 668)

I feel certain that Martin Lings would have affirmed this "fellow witnessing" as an expression of the Divine Mercy which embraces all, and I thank him, even now, for the humble submission that enabled him to be its conduit in my life.

Nancy Roberts
Amman, Jordan

As I Put Down Martin Lings' Book,
I Made a Short Prayer that God Bless This Man.
The Next Day, I Learned of His Passing.

One of the dreadful things about this world now is the ease with which we can go through a day and not feel the dimming of light. Our sense of sacred connection is so co-opted by Starbuck casualness, essential spiritual accoutrements within us are disabled from perceiving the depth of loss that humanity suffered recently with the passing of Martin Lings. In Islamic tradition (and I'm pretty sure the tradition is widespread), when a great person dies, whether a saint or scholar or sage, the whole world is somehow affected, even the fish in the sea.

The night before Dr. Lings passed, I happened to have been reading one of his books that my wife had ordered and just received, *Symbol and Archetype: A Study in the Meaning of Existence*. Once again, I was awestruck by the ease with which Dr. Lings was able to convey tiers of profundity in a short passage (even one sentence) and to do so with uncanny consistency. His translation of verses from the Quran are, in themselves, masterpieces of High English, which none before him could achieve, and not for lack of trying. As I put down the book, I made a short prayer that God bless this man. The next day, I learned of his passing.

Dr. Lings was among the early lights of my life. More than two decades ago, I read his gripping narrative on the life of the Prophet, *Muhammad: His Life Based on the Earliest Sources*. I remember reading almost all of it in one sitting. Had it not been for my need to sleep, I would not have stopped. Shortly thereafter, though, I finished, and when I put the book down I finally understood what it meant to "taste the sweetness" in having love of the Prophet and of prophethood in general. It would be but the first book of Dr. Lings that would be transforming.

A University of Chicago graduate student, whose first name is Ibrahim, handed me Dr. Lings' book, *A Sufi Saint of the Twentieth Century*. He told me, "Read this. You'll like it." I didn't touch the book until a couple of years ago, about 21 years later, in fact. I then started. No exaggeration, it took me a full year to read it. It was so packed, I could not dare dishonor it with cursory handling. I compare the experience with a long epiphany. For some months, before being accosted by the world again, it was hard for me to look at things the same flat way that our era trains us to do. Purpose was everywhere, hidden right there in plain sight.

The "tyranny of quantity" once again shows its cracks: one man inspiring so many to reclaim the esoteric and also to love the Last Prophet. The *sābiqūn* (the foremost in faith and certitude) are few in our times, as the Quran says. It seems that they're even fewer now.

I end this very short personal tribute as I started, with an indictment of the ethos of the times: the shame of our day is the postmodern flattening of existence, the demotion of anything special, anything transcending and capable of a lasting narrative. We're trapped in the glorified Soup Cans of Andy Warhol, his canvas celebration of banality and caustic attempt at making what is ordinary appear special.

God's mercy be upon Dr. Lings.

Ibrahim N. Abusharif
Starlatch Press
Chicago, Illinois

A GENTLE SOUL

I remember purchasing a small metaphysical treatise by an author with a foreign name way back in 1976 as I was browsing the shelves in a small spiritual bookstore located amidst a beautiful garden in Ojai, California. The title was *"The Book of Certainty: The Sufi Doctrine of Faith, Vision and Gnosis,"* and the author was Abu Bakr Siraj ad-Din. At the time, I knew nothing of Islam let alone who the author was, yet the title intrigued me. It was, in essence, what I was searching for—certainty.

I read as much of the book as I could but recall not understanding very much. It quoted extensively from the Quran and offered highly esoteric commentaries in a language quite foreign to me. I set it aside, but my curiosity had been piqued and shortly thereafter, in a life-altering transaction, I purchased a Quran and began to read a very personal revelation that would compel me to convert to the religion of Islam.

After more than a decade abroad seeking sacred knowledge, I returned to the United States and was soon teaching courses on Islam. Not long after I was asked to teach a series of lectures based upon the life of the Prophet, peace be upon him. I agreed but needed a text in English for the students. I began looking for a sound biography of the Prophet that was written in an English style that did justice to the story.

Surprisingly, for a man who the American historian Michael Hart ranked the single most influential human being who every lived, hardly any biographical literature was available other than poorly written works published in far-off places or polemics and misrepresentations. I was somewhat despondent and then I discovered the finely produced *Muhammad: his life based on the earliest sources* by Martin Lings. I knew who he was because I had been warned that I should be careful when reading his books. What I didn't know at the time was that Dr. Martin Lings and Abu Bakr Siraj ad-Din, the man whose book led me to the Quran, were one and the same person. Nevertheless, I decided to read the book and assess it for myself.

I was quickly immersed in a story told by a master story-teller whose English oft-times sang and always soared. The Prophet's life was masterfully narrated through a series of short chapters in a prose as engaging and poetic as Lytton Strachey's in *Eminent Victorians*, only the subject matter was not on an eminent Victorian, but rather written by one who appeared to be. My father, a fine critic of English literature, remarked after reading it that unfortunately the prejudice Westerners have for the topic has prevented it from being recognized as one of the great biographies of the English language.

The book had such a profound impact on my life that I adopted it for the class I was about to teach. In preparation I read it several times, making extensive notes and checked references to the original sources quite often. I was astounded at the historical accuracy of the text and the providential care so evident in the author's choice of versions as well as the underlying structure of the story as he chose to tell it. He followed closely the work of Ibn Hisham but augmented it with several other historical sources.

For those who attended the class, it was an indelible experience marked by the grace that pervaded it, as well as the tears that flowed frequently. I attribute this to the topic of the course, but also to the wonderful presentation of the material in Dr. Lings' book. The lectures were later produced as a tape set and were widely appreciated throughout the United States, Canada, the United Kingdom, and even as far away as Pakistan and Malaysia.

I later came into contact with a few of Dr. Lings' students in the United Kingdom who were pleased with the set and suggested that I meet him. I complied, and on my first visit I was accompanied by the well-known Muslim photographer, Sidi Abdal Adheem Sanders, who has made it his mission in life to photograph as many righteous people throughout the world as possible.

When we arrived at Dr. Lings' humble residence in Kent, we entered into a sparse living room; it had subtle but palpable serenity commonly experienced by those who visit people of copious prayer and invocation. I was struck by the surroundings, the absence of furniture in the room and the simple straw matting on the English cottage floor.

A few minutes later, Dr. Lings, well over ninety years of age, entered the room slowly yet gracefully, greeted us, and asked us to sit down. He sat on a small alcove that looked out upon a stunning English garden that I later learned was of his own tending (and in which he is now buried). I spoke of how much his book had influenced me and told him that I had used it as a basis for my class. He thanked me and yet humbly protested that he had never intended to do something as presumptuous as write the Prophet's biography—peace be upon him— but having been prevailed upon by others finally relented. When I told him of my father's remark, he replied that of the four levels of English, he had written the work at the highest one— far from a boast it was uttered as simple statement of fact from a man who had a degree in medieval English from Oxford, taught

Shakespeare at university for twenty years, and wrote poetry like John Donne!

I then requested a belated permission to teach the book should I do so again in the future. He graciously complied and signed the copy I had brought with me. He began to discuss our present age and how unfortunate it is that people are severed from their spiritual roots. He mentioned how when he had been a child in England, prayer was the lifeblood of the family, and he lamented that many people in England no longer prayed nor even taught their children to do so. He remarked that many people had forgotten that although God is merciful, He nonetheless has a wrathful side and that when people did not actively work to purify themselves, great tribulations came upon them as a result. It seemed, to him, that the world was on the brink of some great purification.

After the meeting, both Sidi Abdal Adheem and I agreed that the presence of the man was not dissimilar to that of some of the righteous men we were fortunate enough to have met in the East. In South Asian culture such a state and the people who possess it are called *hazrat*, derived from the Arabic word for 'presence,' which results from a person's wakefulness achieved through constant remembrance of God.

Another quality that impacted both of us was the utter humility he displayed that was as genuine as the sheepskin rugs he offered us to sit upon. What struck me more than anything else was that during the entire conversation he almost always prefaced his remarks or followed them with a verse from the Quran, which he quoted in eloquent Arabic. His slow and deliberate method of speaking instilled in the listener an anticipation of what was to come as well as a sense that the speaker was acutely aware of the angelic scribes who were anticipating and recording the conversation.

I was happy that I had the good fortune of meeting such a man but lamented that I had never bothered to visit him before. In the weeks that followed, several things that he had mentioned in our hour-long conversation returned to occupy my thoughts, particularly some insights into the Quran that he had brought to my attention. I vowed that if I were in England again, I would try to visit him once more.

Our next meeting came shortly after the first. This time though I was in the company of Habib 'Ali al-Jifry, the well-known scholar and inviter to Islam from Yemen, and a small group of friends. I had known Habib 'Ali for several years and he had desired to see Dr. Lings after being told of him by Fuad Nahdi, publisher of Q-News International. Habib 'Ali has an immense respect for elders and especially for those who have served the Prophet in some way. When he heard of the excellent book Dr. Lings had penned and his love for the Prophet, he desired to visit him with us.

The day that we arrived at the doorsteps of Dr. Lings' abode it was overcast and the atmosphere had an English wetness about it. This time, the good doctor welcomed us at the door and I attributed this to Dr. Lings' impeccable comportment with a direct descendent of the Prophet, and God knows best. He led us to the same room as before and offered us to sit. Habib 'Ali sat closest to Dr. Lings, and I sat next to Habib 'Ali.

Before speaking, Dr. Lings apologized to us and explained that, while during his time in Egypt, he had become quite fluent in Arabic, unfortunately since his return to England his spoken Arabic had been neglected and become quite rusty from lack of use but that he would do his best. To our surprise, he began to speak a very mellifluous classical Arabic that impressed both Habib Ali—who happens to be a master orator in Arabic—and me.

In my subsequent meetings with Dr. Lings, the issue of Perennialism did not arise nor was I inclined to mention it. My respect for his scholarship, discernable spirituality and metaphysical insights not to mention the fact he was more than twice my age in years and three times my age in Islam all demanded I listen attentively to his wisdom and learn from his character. He was a highly educated Muslim, who as the head of Oriental manuscripts at the British Museum, had spent much of his adult life reading some of the finest Arabic manuscripts every put to pen by Muslims and was entirely aware of the orthodox position and had read much finer arguments than I would be able to muster up. I chose to set aside the position I was taught and still adhere to and benefit from a unique English Muslim sage in a bereft and derelict age of folly. As Dr. Lings was a man who spoke when he had something to say and said things that resulted from intense deliberation, I took copious notes on all of my visits.

In my third and final visit to his home, we largely discussed his own poetry and the nature of the poetic muse as well as the importance of poetry for the preservation of language. We ventured into some other interesting areas that are fully expounded upon in some of the Doctor's writings. Last year I attended an extraordinary lecture he gave on 'Shakespeare and Islam' at the Globe Theatre in London. I was asked to introduce Dr. Lings and in doing so I was afforded the extraordinary opportunity to thank him publicly for being the means by which Allah had guided me to Islam and for that I am eternally indebted to him.

He would later apologize for his physical enervation at the talk, but age, he said, was taking its toll. I was struck by the sincere humility of this man and his self-effaced character. My mother, who had attended from America, told me that she had never met anyone with such a transcendent presence as Dr. Lings. She later ordered his book on the Prophet, which I subsequently found by her bedside.

At the Globe Theater, Dr. Lings had been signing books for some people, and when the Moroccan ambassador asked for an inscription, he changed from writing with his left hand to using his right. Apologizing for the poor penmanship, he said he refused to write Arabic with his left hand out of deference to the sacred script.

On speaking with a close friend of Dr. Lings who had known him for over fifty years, I learned that the man had been an atheist and that, upon meeting Dr. Lings, had rediscovered his faith because, for the first time in his life, he felt he had met a genuinely pious man of God. He eventually embraced Islam at Dr. Lings' hand and was still close to him after several decades, with only increased admiration.

Dr. Martin Lings became a Muslim in 1938, partly, he told me, because he felt that Islam was unique among the world religions in maintaining transmission in its revelation as well as in its sciences, through unbroken chains that involved a "handing down," the literal meaning of tradition.

He performed the Hajj in 1939 and explained to me that his parents had helped finance his pilgrimage; he also mentioned that upon arriving by ship at the port at Jeddah from Sudan, he was asked by the *ad hoc* customs agents if he was Muslim. He replied that he was, and they asked him for proof. To this, he recited to them the simple creed of Islam that guarantees the right of anyone who utters it in the presence of witnesses the title Muslim, "*Ashadu an La ilaha illa ʾLlah, wa ashadu anna Muhammadan rasulu ʾLlah!*" They asked him for some more proof, at which point he looked at them and said, "What proof do you have that you are Muslim?" They let him in.

His last public act was to celebrate the life of our beloved Prophet, peace be upon him, at Wembly Conference Center in London. Habib 'Ali and I were invited to participate as well.

Before Dr. Lings spoke he was given a highly warranted lifetime achievement award for his dedication in spreading the message of peace and love embodied in Islam. In his short talk he spoke of the gift the Prophet was and of the Prophet's active engagement with his community and what a great blessing that was for us. Dr. Lings left us with the subtle thought that the Messenger is still with us. He left the hall immediately after speaking.

I knew that he must have been tired and I felt gratitude to have seen him again. I had shaken his hand and thanked him for a remarkable reflection not knowing at the time I was looking into his gentle and serene face for the last time.

My speech, which followed his, had been a result of something that he had raised in his talk. The next day, Dr. Lings, who I now called Sidi Abu Bakr, attempted to call me, and when I returned his call he assured me that he wanted to attend my talk but was exhausted. He had called to reassure himself that I took no offense at his early departure. On the contrary, I replied, I was very happy that he could attend the conference and was deeply moved by his words. He then told me that he had not mentioned all that he had wished to say in this talk, as he feared that perhaps people would misunderstand.

He told me that he was greatly struck by the Prophet's current involvement with his community, as Muslims around the world saw him in their dreams and derived spiritual sustenance from his vision. Moreover, he said that when writing his book, *Muhammad,* he was overwhelmed with the presence of the Prophet during the entire time and felt a great blessing in having been able to complete it.

After some time on the phone, he said, "I am so sorry for carrying on so long; please excuse me." I realized I was speaking to a man who embodied the prophetic character. I was not interested in whatever differences we might have in abstruse points of creed; I wanted only to learn from his gentle and upright manner.

Dr. Lings was a man of small physical stature, as if God had created him to be close to the earth he loved and tended, but he was a celestial intellectual and spiritual giant in an age of dwarfed terrestrial aspirations and endeavors.

Dr. Lings once told me that the problem with the modern Muslim is egocentricity, but that true Islam is Theo-centric: it puts God, not oneself, at the center of life. I believe Dr. Lings was a true Muslim, a man who put God at the center of his life and purpose.

I feel immensely honored to have known him and to have benefited from his knowledge through his books and his presence.

May Allah have mercy on his soul and sanctify his secret.

Hamza Yusuf
Danville, California

Postscript: I wrote this after learning of Dr. Lings' death this morning. Returning to my home I found a package marked "urgent." I asked my wife when had it arrived, and she informed me that it came today. I opened it and found, to my utter surprise, a pre-publication copy of Dr. Lings' final book, that I had not even known he had written, entitled *A Return to the*

Spirit. On the inside of the cover-piece was this message: "Dr. Lings requested you by name to write something for the back of the book!" I sat down and read the short book without being able to put it down, as it was an extended exposition on the very topics we had discussed in our meetings. Upon finishing, I felt as if I had received a wonderful personal letter from a man who was the means by which I was guided and who I had come to love for the sake of God. While I believe in some ways that event was a *karamah* from God at the hands of the Sidi Abu Bakr Siraj ad-Din, his real *karamah* was his impeccable character, piety and uprightness of action in all aspects of his life. May God shower him in His grace and mercy.

Written May 12, 2005

In Memoriam

I was first introduced to Sidi Abu Bakr Siraj ad-Din through his book, *Muhammed: his life based on the earliest sources*, by Martin Lings. Although I had known the Prophet's story as it was recounted to me countless times during my childhood, the manner in which it was portrayed by the "English Gentleman" was very moving. When I later enthusiastically read some of his writings, what struck me was the clarity with which Sidi Abu Bakr wrote. It truly takes an enlightened spirit to explain centuries-old and seemingly complex concepts with such clarity for virtually anyone to understand. Dr. Martin Lings (Sidi Abu Bakr Siraj ad-Din) was able to do it so beautifully, touching us with his translucence and awakening our hearts forever.

H.R.H. Princess Nafa'a Ali bin Nayef
Amman, Jordan

About Dr. Lings

My childhood was filled with the wondrous world of the fairy tales and fables. Among the characters of those stories was often a sage. As I had not met any sages in real life, I just assumed they only existed in stories of "once upon a time." My heart was filled with joy when in my early twenties I met a few sages, Dr. Lings among them. When Dr. Lings spoke, I would be transported to a timeless age and drink of the fountain of Wisdom from which his words came. How wonderful it was to gaze at him and listen to him! How fortunate and grateful I am to have met him!

Glória de Barros
Campinas, Brazil

A LIFE FOR CERTAINTY

For many people Martin Lings' death last May 12th, at the age of ninety-six, is the disappearance of a protagonist of the "traditional" thought. With him passes away the last one of the first generation of those who have witnessed and contributed to the birth, in the last century, of a "perennialist" vision of Sacred Civilizations in the West.

The concept of a unique and universal Tradition called in Islam the *Dīn al-Qayyim* has been at the substratum of all his writings. This emerges, for instance, in *Ancient Beliefs and Modern Superstitions* (1964), a small work of his mature thought where the acute genius of Lings expresses itself thoroughly. With mastery and simplicity, but at the same time with brilliant expression and deep intuition, he accompanies the reader in discovering that perfection which has been the intrinsic nature of the original condition of humanity. In it, with wise illustrations, he shows us what separates altogether an archaic civilization founded upon the contemplation of unchangeable truths, where all is a manifestation of qualitative synthesis, from the modern one, where every thing develops itself without an immovable centre of constant orientation, without a vision regulating in a harmonic way the chaotic growth of its ephemeral productions.

Credo ut intelligam, intelligo ut credam, wrote St. Augustine. The match of these two propositions perfectly applied to Martin Lings who has not only been the intense spirit of an intellectual and a researcher, but also - and I would say above all - a Believer, in the fuller sense of the term, one that

121

has testified with his words, deeds and writings the contents of the light deposited in his heart.

Having been a dedicated Muslim for the majority of his long life, where he was known with the name of Abu Bakr Sirāj al-Dīn, his main concern was naturally devoted to showing the truth and beauty of the Eternal Wisdom as it has been mirrored in traditional and esoteric Islam. Conscious, as he was, of the ineluctable finality of its Message, he spent a great deal of his efforts to show to the contemporary West, a secular West that seems distracted and absent to every call toward unchangeable truths, the deep face of the last one among the great sacred civilizations.

Nourished at the everlasting spring of the inner meaning of the Divine Word and the Sunna (or Traditions and Sayings) of the Prophet ﷺ, as reflected also by his personal involvement in the teachings and methods of Sufism, Lings knew how to communicate with elegance the intrinsic harmony and the mysterious depth of the Perennial Wisdom. Without doubt, of this Wisdom he has been one of the most excellent interpreters within the different trends of the "traditionalist" school which goes back, as everybody knows, to the work of René Guénon, that Lings knew and frequented for a long time. Although Lings did always recognize the weight and the importance of the illustrious French metaphysician in his own thought, he however maintained a certain autonomy in relation to Guénon on some doctrinal points.

Coming now to the numerous works of Islamic content written by Lings, we can not fail to mention the brief but dense work *The Book of Certainty* (1952), based on the *Ta'wīlāt al-Qur'ān*, the esoteric commentary of Qāshānī in the Koran, written at an early age during the years of his stay in Cairo (1939-1952); nor his *A Sufi Saint of the Twentieth Century* (1961), that gives us an attractive hagiographical and doctrinal image of the Shadhili saint of Mustaghanem, the Sheikh Ahmad al-'Alawī (1869-1934), whose spiritual irradiation, also in the western world, has widely influenced the spiritual renewal of the contemporary Islamic world; nor can be forgotten *The Quranic Art of Calligraphy and Illumination* (1976), written on the occasion of the World of Islam Festival in London, which introduces us to the underlying symbolic framework of Koranic calligraphy, where the beauty of Islamic art reaches its zenith. But his undisputed masterpiece remains the splendid biography of the Prophet Muhammad ﷺ, for which he received international awards from the Islamic world.

I remember when, talking with his English publisher before the work was completed, he told me how much Lings not only worried that the spiritual image of the Prophet ˘ might not come to light, but also about external detail such as ascertaining if in his eye there had been a vein or a stain of red. This detail was not included in the final version of the book, but this shows us how his concern in verifying the least details concerning the Model of every believer was present in his heart. The subtitle of the Prophet's biography: *His Life Based on the Earliest Sources* is, alone, the guarantee of the traditional authoritativeness of this work, and is perhaps the most influential factor in presenting the right image of the Prophet of Islam ˘ and more importantly, for encouraging love for him outside Islamic countries.

Now that the Curtain has been lifted, we like to think that Lings, too—paraphrasing a well known saying of *Sayyidna* 'Alī—"might have found greater Certainty."

Paolo Urizzi
Viaso, Italy

In Memoriam

Sidi Abu Bakr is a gentle, loving, forgiving and generous soul who through his journey on earth touched whoever met him with radiant compassion and will continue to do so from his next life.

Princess Wijdan Ali
Amman, Jordan

WITH DR. MARTIN LINGS AT MACCHU PICCHU

The place was the shrine of the Peruvian Saint Rosa de Lima (1586-1617), patroness of all Latin America, and, in fact, the first canonized saint of the continent. It was a cold morning in August 1985. This was the time and place of my first meeting with this completely out-of-the-ordinary human being, the late Dr. Martin Lings.

My wife, myself, and a group of friends from Brazil, were in Lima for a conference on religion held by the *Instituto de Estudios Tradicionales* of Peru. As a traditional Catholic-*cum*-Traditionalist, I thought it was an auspicious sign that Dr. Martin Lings, as a prominent spokesman for the Perennial Philosophy, should with much devotion visit the shrine of this disciple of the great St. Catherine of Siena and that it was at such a site that I had the first opportunity to talk to him.

My first impression was that he was a man delicate as silk, calm as a swan, alert like an Andean condor, thin as a greyhound and at the same time firm like a cathedral.

I had then read only two of his books and intended to translate *Ancient Beliefs and Modern Superstitions*, since I believed the book would make an excellent partner for and sequel to Guénon's *Crisis of the Modern World* for the Portuguese-reading public. Dr Lings received me then with much courtesy and interest and gave me his agreement for the translation of his work, which I did immediately upon my return home (subsequently it was published by Polar, in São Paulo).

On the return journey from the Santa Rosa shrine to the conference site, I had the opportunity of sitting beside him in the bus and so we could talk freely for a good time. *Festina lente* ("hasten slowly," "do it quickly, but calmly") was a *motto* that I thought would fit him well, for he seemed to be the calmest man in the world and at the same time he was rather rapid when circumstances obliged.

In his lectures at the Lima seminar, he expounded traditional wisdom with clarity and precision, and criticized with candor the errors of the modern mentality. When speaking, he seemed to grow in size; when expounding universal Truth, he seemed to reach the dimension of a giant on the stage of the conference room; Truth, I later discovered, has the capacity of transforming men into giants. Transfigured by Truth, he was as it were able to hypnotize the audience with the power of the knowledge and presence of the sacred.

At the end of the lectures in the seaside Capital of Peru, we climbed almost three thousand meters in order to reach the "old summit" of Macchu Picchu. It was there, in the last stronghold of the Incan civilization, that we had the second opportunity of meeting Dr. Lings. Hidden in the mountains and known only to the elite of the Incas, Macchu Picchu was a kind of "esoteric" city, hidden in the high altitudes from mundane curiosity. Because of this, and also because of the fact that its religion constituted a branch of the "primordial tradition", it was highly symbolic for us.

Despite the fact that Dr. Lings was already 76 years old then—and the oldest person in a group of lecturers that included Joseph Epes Brown, Rama Coomaraswamy, Victor Danner, Gai Eaton, S.H. Nasr and Huston Smith, amongst others—he surprised his companions in the excursion with his agility and resistance. He was always the first to climb a hill or to face stairs of a thousand steps. In the beginning of the tour, Rama Coomaraswamy, a medical doctor, expressed his concern about the physical health of Dr. Lings, especially at such a high altitude. Dr. Coomaraswamy intended to walk alongside his senior companion, to make sure that (physically speaking) everything was going well for him. But very soon he gave up his mission. The fact was that he simply could not keep in pace with Dr. Lings. Neither Coomaraswamy nor any of the others could walk up the hills as fast as the oldest man in the group. And it seemed that he never got tired. Dr. Lings was in better shape than all of us!

During the tour, he made the singular remark that the butterflies of the Southern Hemisphere were more friendly than the ones from the Northern Hemisphere. He was a master of comparative religion and a man engaged in pure metaphysics, so it surprised a neophyte like myself to hear such a person utter a commentary in the field of what, for want of a better term, one could call "comparative zoology". In fact, the delicate insects seemed to approach him without fear. Perhaps he wanted to indicate that even the animal world responds in its own way to the pressures and futile agitations of the modern world—that is to say, the less modernized and industrialized a place is, the more "friendly" are its inhabitants, even if they be butterflies!

I had the privilege of speaking to Martin Lings for the last time just a few months before his passage to the *champs Élysées*, I telephoned him regarding the publication in Brazil of his book on Shakespeare. He gave me a good interview which was published in *O Estado de São Paulo*, the second largest Brazilian paper. In the interview he said some things of which I had previously been unaware, for instance, the interest of Guénon in Shakespeare and the support he gave to Lings regarding his insights about the esoteric dimension of the bard's plays.

My wife and I visited him once in his lovely cottage in the outskirts of London. There he received us with his proverbial hospitality and generosity. He seemed to us the most humble and generous of men, and this was combined with a powerful will and intelligence. He was a lively example of a harmonious combination of strength and suavity. In São Paulo a traditional requiem mass was celebrated for his beautiful soul. *Requiescat in pace.*

Mateus Soares de Azevedo
São Paulo, Brazil
Author of *Iniciación al Islam y Sufismo*
(Barcelona, 2004) and *The Intelligence of Faith* (São Paulo, 2005)

AN INDEBTED LITHUANIAN

Some 18 years ago, Lithuania still was occupied by the Soviet Union and the Communist powers were extremely suspicious as regards any serious religious studies (especially those related to Sufism). The main source of information about Eastern mystical traditions were the illegal underground translations and books produced by the officially recognized Russian Orientalists. As a young scholar of the Lithuanian State Institute of Culture and Arts, which itself belonged to the Lithuanian Academy of Sciences, I had an access to the chief academic libraries in Moscow and was enthusiastically involved in the secret and quite risky task of making photocopies of the rare and otherwise unobtainable English books. I was lucky enough to find a copy of *A Sufi Saint of the Twentieth Century* by Dr. Martin Lings. This book—along with the acquired microfilms which contained different works by F. Schuon and other Traditionalist writers—completely changed my view regarding Sufism, thus enabling me to move away from such authors as Idris Shah, Hazrat Inayat Khan, and Gurdjieff.

After a few years of intense religious studies, when Lithuania was about to gain her independence and when all ties with Moscow were cut off, I wrote a letter to Dr. Martin Lings. I was very surprised and astonished when, after several months passed, one gloomy autumn day the letter of Dr. Martin Lings arrived to our no less gloomy apartment in Vilnius, illuminating it with certain beneficial light. What particularly impressed me, was to learn that Dr. Martin Lings himself used to live in Lithuania before II World War and the Soviet invasion, lecturing at the Vytautas Magnus University in Kaunas for a couple of years.

During the most difficult period of chaos which followed the end of the Soviet occupation, Dr. Martin Lings used to send me various books, also encouraging me by maintaining a regular correspondence for about three years. In 1992, when the situation in Lithuania turned really disastrous, Dr. M. Lings invited me to visit him in England and paid all my expenses of travel and stay. It was amazing, that he personally met me at the Gatwick airport. At that time, Dr. M. Lings still remembered some Lithuanian words and was able to sing the Lithuanian folk songs. Due to this visit which lasted one month, a permanent relationship was established with numerous friends in England. The providential kindness of Dr. M. Lings manifested itself in two main respects: first and foremost, he, as a spiritual guide, showed me the Sufi path; second, through the regular financial support he saved me from the real perdition which threatened me and my family in the post-Communist Lithuania. In January 2005, I met Dr. M. Lings for the last time in Amman, Jordan, where I stayed at the American Center of Oriental Research, being granted the Andrew W. Mellon Fellowship award. From the time of our first encounter, Dr. M. Lings was and still remains the central and exceptional figure in my spiritual life, my thoughts and my feelings.

Assoc. Prof. Dr. Algis Uzdavinys
Kaunas, Lithuania

On the News of Lings' Departure to the Other World

There are phenomena in every life that defy the kind of logic usually relied upon by most people. It would seem as if the human will, using reason to determine action, could achieve just about anything. But, sifting through experiences with the hindsight of over forty years, one has to admit that very little has been driven by human will. The same goes for teachers and friends. They are sent to us from somewhere and if we wonder from where and why, what is revealed again is the Secret, in such a way that all words originate from and return to It.

A long time ago, during one of Sarajevo's summers, when my wife, Halida, returned from visiting her uncle in London, she brought with her several books, and through these books, meetings commenced with Martin Lings. Letters and conversations exchanged with him and with several of his friends could, I thought, God willing, turn into a book. This very book now ends with the news of the departure, not long after midnight on 12 May 2005, of Sidi Abu Bakr's departure to the other world, a world which, through the whole experience of friendship with him, was always reflected in the warmth of his voice and actions. Taken together with the sacred art which Sidi Abu Bakr was dedicated to throughout his life, this reflection of human goodness is the most important testament to the holy tradition.

I have translated his book *What is Sufism?* in the solitude of my Panonian retreats. Although it comes from the farthest depths of the self, it directly explains the destructiveness of ideological images—as are found in Communism. But a "self" yearning to be located in the Self requires the opposite: away from all that exists—the material, the imaginary and the ordered world—to return to that which lies beyond any representation. Our dear Professor Lings testified to this from the center of being that is the "site" of the beginning and the return. It is from this "site" that all people separate and come back as friends.

And later, during the siege of Sarajevo and the war against Bosnia, when all purpose seemed to be lost, by candlelight and gas lamps, with the sounds of bombardment and the smell of smoke in the burning city, together with Edin, Halida, and Amra, while the children sheltered in the safe places in the apartment, we translated the book *Muhammad: His Life based on the Earliest Sources*. All the dilemmas of the Prophet and the people surrounding him, arising from their contact with the Revelation, were like a whiteness through which all records of human sufferings could be gleaned. Spending time with Lings in this way helped me to transcend the conditioned self and transient time in search of comprehensive answers to questions about the meaning of the world and human beings.

The two books I mentioned were born in the Bosnian language, as if from its depths, from the place where Oneness has revealed its power to unify and harmonise all differences. All that has been yearned for through the centuries and admired in the Bosnian ideal, has been situated in the Oneness that is both reflected and contained in multiplicity. No ideological project, designed to grasp and maintain such unity in diversity, has resulted in salvation. Quite the contrary. It seemed that the power of ideologies was killing off Bosnian unity in diversity.

Bosnian editions of Lings' books were designed by the graphic designer Dzevad Hozo. In Hozo's graphics, Martin Lings would recognize something he found in calligraphy. This meeting between the writer and the graphic designer in Bosnia speaks of the proximity of the Secret.

In our last conversation Lings told me, as he had often done, of his life, his first encounters with Réne Guénon and Titus Burkhardt and of his new book *A Return to the Spirit*. He described each of the chapters. I had expected to receive a copy of the book from him, but, instead, I got a letter, handwritten as always, telling me that his visit to Bosnia was unlikely. So, our last conversation was about *A Return to the Spirit*. It is only in this way that comings and goings occur where it would seem impossible, in a world that does not reveal the Face. For everything disappears but the Face of God.

Rusmir Mahmutcehajic
Sarajevo, Bosnia

In Memoriam

Shaykh Abu Bakr Siraj ad-Din (Martin Lings) was one of those rare beings who became an example of the life that the Prophet Muhammad spoke of and represented. He found the key to happiness and spirituality in this life in the Name of Allah, which he invoked constantly, and through his presence inspired others to do the same.

Shems Friedlander
The American University of Cairo, Egypt

Shaykh Abu Bakr (Dr. Martin Lings): A Reminiscence of Cairo Days

It was a troubled young man who arrived in Cairo in October, 1950. After three years spent in Jamaica, I had returned to London to seek work and found myself unemployable. Finally one of many job applications bore fruit and I was appointed an Assistant Lecturer in the English Department of Cairo University on the strength of having had a book on Hindu Vedanta, Taoism, and Zen published. While still in Jamaica I had received several letters asking why I had never mentioned Islam in my book. Back in London I had met two of these correspondents, members of a Sufi *ṭarīqah* to which, as it happened, Martin Lings also belonged. They had written to tell him of his new colleague.

On my first morning at the University he was not there so I asked a student about him. "That," I was informed, "is the gentleman who speaks to the flowers and who is much loved." The following day I met him, a small, wiry man twelve years my senior. This was the beginning of a friendship which endured until his death 55 years later. He and his wife were living in a dusty village at the foot of the Pyramids, their home set in a lush walled garden which seemed like a little paradise. Desperately homesick for Jamaica, it was certainly a paradise for me, a refuge in which I was always welcome. Lings or Sidi Abu Bakr as I soon learned to call him was a source of astonishment to me. Brought up as an agnostic I had never before met anyone "religious," let alone a man of deep and unshakeable faith who pursued a spiritual path with total dedication.

There were numerous handsome cats prowling the paradise-garden. Without, of course, believing in "reincarnation" as the concept is commonly understood, Sidi Abu Bakr drew inspiration from the Quranic verse which tells us that the birds and the beasts are *communities like to yourselves and to Him they are returned*. He believed that the animal soul derives huge benefits from close association with human creatures who fulfill, in prayer, their viceregal function. His kittens were much in demand but he refused to give them to any family that did not pray regularly. I soon began to share his sensibilities, understanding, for example, his hatred of the public loud speakers which blared Quranic recitation, distorting the sacred words in a manner almost blasphemous, a symptom of a naïve and pathetic worship of technology in the Arab world.

I witnessed also the devotion of his students who sensed his profound faith and were influenced by it in their own lives. He was a marvelous teacher, particularly when he shared with them his love of Shakespeare. Every year he produced and directed one of the great plays, drawing excellent performances from the student cast. A perfectionist, he expected the best from them and achieved this, not by bullying but by gentle coaxing and by imbuing them with something of his own unique understanding of the spiritual depth of meaning in these plays.

He had, at this time, just completed his first book, *The Book of Certainty*, and I read it in draft. It opened my eyes to the power and beauty of Islam as did all that he told me of his "spiritual grandfather" in the *silsilah* of his Tariqah, the Algerian Shaikh al-'Alawi whose biography he would write some years later. Above all his companionship made me feel that I could be at home in the House of Islam. I might have postponed indefinitely the decision to take the next step but, after less than a year in Cairo, I decided to return to Jamaica and realised that it was a matter of "now or never." In 1951, in the month of Ramadan, I went to him and said I was ready to take the *shahada* at his hands. It was as a Muslim that I boarded a ship in Alexandria, a penniless deck passenger, just three weeks later.

Hasan Gai Eaton

In Memory of Shaykh Abu Bakr Siraj ad-Din,
in abiding gratitude and love

It must have been in April 1960 when I was first ushered into his office in the British Museum. This short, thin, bearded man stood up behind his desk and extended his hand to me. There was a slight but welcoming smile on his face as he said, "Please, sit down". His hair was not yet gray and came down over his ears somewhat. Although this was the first time I had seen him, it seems now, as I look back, that I was most struck by his eyes. I did not have the impression of being looked at, even on the rare occasion that our eyes met; his vision seemed to be focused elsewhere. And yet his eyes seemed to gleam somehow, even in full daylight.

Some four years later, at a *majlis* in London, over which he presides, we were all eating an uncooked meal, as was the custom. On such evenings, he took care never to overeat. He carefully ate only one and a half slices of brown bread with butter and cheese, a small piece of cake, with perhaps an extra half piece of fruit.

One of the *fuqara* asked him something like, "Isn't it terrible that scientists are sending more and more rockets into space, and they plan to even land something on the moon?" He did not answer immediately, his head was bowed as he carefully cut his slice of bread. He raised his head and looked toward the *faqir* who had spoken. Eyes gleaming, he replied,

"Perhaps what young people are doing these days may be more displeasing to God on High than the scientists who want to send a rocket to the moon."

During the early sixties I used to visit him every second week at the British Museum. On one such occasion he related to me that he had a Christian minister friend who used to see him in Cairo. This minister told him one day that the Sura al-Fatiha (Opening Chapter of Qur'an) was the most perfect prayer he had ever read. He then said to me, "Indeed, the Sura al-Fatiha says everything that we could want to say to God."

I'm not sure of the year but it was before 1965. I was invited with Sidi Salman to the Lings' home for dinner in outer London. They usually invited us twice a month, they were very generous to us. After the meal we were all sitting in the front room in silent invocation of God. I was sitting diagonally across from him when suddenly he gasped out loud. I hesitatingly opened my eyes to look at him. His head was held high under a white turban, his eyes closed. His noble face held an amazing expression of beauty and awe which I have never forgotten. Later, during the prayer, he recited the Verses of Light, as he often did. When we entered the prostration his voice was very faint, but filled with awe and reverence, as he whispered, "God is most Great."

I would like to add a couple of anecdotes, concerning this great man, which might be of interest:

In England, when he sat the final examinations for his Arabic degree it was Ramadan. As it was May, the fast lasted from before 4 a.m. until after 8 p.m. The examinations were taken in a large hall; rain was beating down on the roof as he waited for the examination paper. As he turned it over, a single drop of rain fell onto the top of the paper. I recall his joyful and yet humble smile when he recalled, "At that moment I knew everything was going to be alright." His marks were very high; he completed his studies one year ahead of the time usually allocated.

As a young student at Oxford, he read Plato's Cave Allegory. He told us, "Our professor came into the class and said to us, 'Before we begin, I want you to know that what you are about to read is one of the greatest things which has ever been written.'" As he was saying this his eyes opened wide, he looked upwards somewhat, they filled with that gaze of majesty and awe. Seeing this, I lowered my own gaze.

With these few extracts I've tried to show something of this man of God, may God be well-pleased with him.

Mansur Murray

Oijda Valley, Morocco

REMINISCENCES OF A GREAT MAN OF THE SPIRIT
OF THE TWENTIETH AND BEGINNING
OF THE TWENTY-FIRST CENTURIES

"There where thy Treasure is, there will thy heart be." This golden sentence summarizes Martin Lings' love for the true, the sacred and the beautiful, and his total immersion in this path. He who, at the "eleventh hour" of his life, already radiated the light and love of the hereafter. It did not take his passing away for the perfume of sanctity to be felt in the herebelow— those who had the blessing to be close to him can testify to it. The gate of his heart was open to the luminous work of his sanctified soul. He was a spiritual aristocrat, a Sufi of the path of *Ma'rifah*—knowledge

The sense of the sacred, the true, and the beautiful led him from an early age to things of the spirit. This spiritual dimension dominated his whole life, and guided him to meet Frithjof Schuon, a beacon of wisdom and certitude and the greatest writer of the last century, as Lings himself attested. From this guide and friend—in the deepest sense—Lings found the path to the Treasure of treasures, the path he traveled for over 60 years with all his heart, with all his soul, with all his strength.

In every spirituality, the passing of the beads of a rosary symbolizes the spiritual life. The cord-axis that unites the beads symbolizes the transcendent Truth and the Sacred. The beads themselves symbolize particularly: virtues, prayer or invocation, therefore conformity to the Truth and the Sacred. The beauty of soul that we saw in this great man—a gardener of his character whose spiritual work radiated like the flowers he

grew—that soul shone with the virtues of detachment, efface-
ment and humility; vigilance and perseverance; patience and
resignation; faith, fervor and trust; discrimination, certitude of
the absolute reality, and serenity of spirit; and finally the one
virtue or beauty of soul that unites them all, that is, inwardness.
This is the soul's opening to the gate of the Heart, to the Treasure of treasures, where it is God who prays in us, if it is permitted to express oneself thus. It is the union of soul and spirit
in Divine Love and Light.

When we heard of his passing away, we felt the need to
attend his funeral, so we started our trip immediately, and after
ten hours of travel we arrived at the Lings' little stone house in
England, a few hours before the funeral. We sat in his room in
quiet recollection, immersed in this holy ambience, and then
one by one his close friends arrived from England and abroad.
Their faces showed a combination of deep grief and serenity,
for a beloved friend and guide was departing, one who will be
very much missed. At the same time, the reality of the spiritual
graces filled the air around us, and it could not be otherwise,
for a holy man was being taken to the hereafter. Mercy to him
who has lived a perfected life at the heights of wisdom and
sanctity.

The solemn ceremony took place in his own garden, one of
the most beautiful we have ever seen, and every flower bush
was in bloom with yellows, ochres, reds and shades of blues,
with a backdrop of green hills, meadows and forests. That
morning the sky was a deep blue and the sun was shining, seemingly with the joy of Heaven opening its gates; in the afternoon, the wind blew in white clouds first, then the skies closed,
prayers were said, sacred texts read, his body was enthroned
among the flowers and in mother earth's bosom, but his soul
rose to the sky, and celestial beings came to take it, this I did
see with the eye of my heart. A holy ground this place will
remain. We must briefly render homage and express our heart-
felt gratitude to Mrs. Lings, because behind every great man
there is always a loving and self-effaced woman. Without her,
things would not have been the same. Our prayers and love are
also with her.

Upon our return home, we felt compelled to read Lings' book, *The Eleventh Hour*. We mentioned the virtue of inwardness above, the synthesis of all other virtues. In his book, he says: "'The kingdom of Heaven is within you.' This truth is the basis of esoterism, the science and discipline of inwardness." Lings has shown us by his exemplary life that it was inspired by essential truths such as expressed in the above-quoted phrase from the Bible. What he wrote about he practiced. In wisdom "to know" becomes "to be," and in sanctity "to be" is "to know." We are most inspired by men like him, who represent the best possibilities of human kind even at the "eleventh hour" of the macrocosm. We see in him the results of the compensatory aspects at the end of time; these positive aspects counterbalance the disadvantages for the true seeker of pure spirituality. In this book Lings presents first the negative aspects of these times in light of tradition and prophecy, then the positive aspects. He demonstrates that the times are far worse, and yet, far better, than they are generally believed to be.

"The corresponding ills of the macrocosm likewise create a climate which is not unfavorable to wisdom on condition that they are seen as ills. Detachment is an essential feature of the sage, this virtue, which in better times could only be acquired through great spiritual efforts, can be made more spontaneous by the sight of one's world in chaotic ruins. There is yet another feature of normal old age, the most positive of all, which likewise has its macrocosmic equivalent, in virtue of which our times are unique. It is sometimes said of spiritual men and women at the end of their lives that they have 'one foot already in Paradise.' This is not to deny that death is a sudden break, a rupture of continuity. It cannot but be so, for it has to transform mortal old age into immortal youth. Nonetheless, hagiography teaches us that the last days of sanctified souls can be remarkably luminous and transparent…the nearness of a new Golden Age cannot fail to make itself mysteriously felt before the end of a new cycle."

May the great silence after his departure be filled with the example he left us, one who followed and found the Treasure, for "where thy Treasure is, there will thy heart be."

Hernán Darío Cadavid Medina
Medellin, Columbia

A Sufi Saint of the 21ˢᵗ Century:

Only a few years (but at that age, very long years) passed from that time in Beirut in the early seventies when I first heard of Shaykh Abu Bakr to that moment in the summer of 1976 when I finally met him. From the beginning, I knew of him as Sidi Abu Bakr Siraj al-Din who was also and quantitatively speaking, better known, as Dr. Martin Lings.

At the time I was a Master's degree candidate concentrating on Islamic Political Thought at the American University in Beirut. The man who introduced me to the Dr. Lings' books was my advisor and professor for most of my graduate courses, Dr. Yusuf Ibish, himself a *faqir,* a disciple of a Sufi shaykh. Sidi Yusuf, as he was known among other *fuqara* (*Sidi* being a respectful and fraternal form of address used within Sufi circles particularly those deriving their practices from North African Sufi tradition) quite early on indicated that there was a *tariqa* (both a spiritual path and a spiritual fraternity or order devoted to that path that roughly approximates a monastic order) that reflected in practice and doctrine the spiritual perspective of Sidi Abu Bakr and that he played an important, and illuminating role within the *tariqa* as well as within the broader and more informal and then quite obscure association of extraordinary writers and thinkers known as the Traditionalist school. This group of metaphysicians who included scholars of sacred art and comparative religion in the most transcendent sense, rejected modernist thought from a perspective equally at home within a broadly orthodox understanding of all of the world's great religions. And through Sidi Yusuf I was fortunate to meet one or two other luminaries of this school and even of this *tariqa*, who deeply impressed me.

But it was two very related events that had the greatest impact, and which I must now recount. By 1976 I was living in Cairo and by then fully aware of the importance of the *turuq* (the overall body of Sufi orders) as the inner core of Islam and even attending the *hadra* (the collective invocation of the Names of God) of various *turuq* active in the Egyptian capital. But I was indecisive about such a potentially decisive moment that my growing interest in Sufism posed.

As Heaven would have it I had the occasion at that time to make my first Haj (the required pilgrimage to Mecca) in the company of dear friends and family. We were camped in tents pitched on top of a hill, Yemeni Hill, in Mena (a hill not far from Mecca that has since been leveled, along with much else in the Hejaz). From our perch above the Mena plains, I saw a party making their way up the hill to our tents. It was Sidi Yusuf—who I knew would also be making this Haj in the company of then Sidi Abu Bakr and other *fuqara*. Indeed, Sidi Yusuf was accompanying Sidi Abu Bakr and when they reached our tent, I was in Sidi Abu Bakr's presence, and the presence of the *Baraka*, the spiritual grace—that attached itself to his presence and was tangible to my soul, if invisible to my eyes.

I thought: For the past few years I have known of this man, this Dr. Martin Lings, above all, as the extraordinary author of a work on the spiritual significance of Shakespeare, and at that moment of my life perhaps even more importantly, as the author of *A Sufi Saint of the 20ᵗʰ Century*. And I thought, yes I understand thanks to Dr. Lings, the importance of the life and legacy of the late Shaykh Ahmed al-Alawi (the subject of this latter book), but here before me at that moment and ever since, this Sidi Abu Bakr al-Siraj ad-Din—was a Living Sufi Saint.

I returned to Cairo, rejoicing in the many wonderful events that had taken place in the Hejaz (the coastal and inland stretch of Western Arabia that includes Mecca, Medina and Jeddah). But I was also perplexed, having difficulties with the published and highly metaphysical work of Sidi Abu Bakr's own Shaykh. Until one day, I returned to Cairo from covering a story outside of Egypt (I worked then as bureau chief and producer-reporter for NBC News) to discover from one of my dearest friends who had also made the Haj, that Sidi Yusuf had been to Cairo during my absence and had left a critical text—actually an excerpt from a letter, written by Shaykh Isa, Sidi Abu Bakr's Shaykh. This, unpublished, brief text stressed the overwhelming imperative that both meaning and triumph over failure in this world was assured at the very moment we understood the great Gift given to us by God in giving us His Supreme Name.

The excerpt goes:

> Human nature is prone to lose sight of the ineffable happiness which lies in the possession of the Name. What bliss to have been born man and, being man, to have obtained the *Dhikr*! The *fuqara* must be told ... Even if one's life had been a failure in every respect, if at this very moment one has the grace of invoking the Supreme Name, all this apparent failure is in reality a life that has been won, nothing is lost; every life would be worth living if it led up to the possibility, at this very moment, even as we think about it, of invoking the Name with Faith. *Wa'Llahu al-Musta'an.*

Later this would be further amplified as well as simplified in a formal text, as two inseparable axioms laid down by Sheikh Ahmed al-Alawi and passed on and commented upon by Shaykh 'Isa and which I have come to understand as the fruit of 1,400 or so years of Sufi meditation upon God and His Prophet. These "two inseparable axioms as the guiding principle of our lives" to quote Shaykh Isa quoting Shaykh Ahmed al-Alawi al Darqawi in a text given to me and also commented upon by Shaykh Abu Bakr:

> God is truly Present in His Name. The soul must conform to that Presence.

But back to that moment reading the first text left for me in Cairo by Sidi Yusuf; my sense of the gentle yet overpowering presence of Sidi Abu Bakr became a consciousness that he was, for me and for others, *the* living witness of these words of Shaykh Isa that disclosed with finality a heart-shuddering yet liberating Mystery. And so he remained, but ever more so, with each passing year until the end.

At his last public appearance before his death Shaykh Abu Bakr addressed an amazing Mauled (a celebration equivalent to the traditional Saint's Day in older times when Europe was still Christian) for the Prophet held in a London suburb, which is particularly significant in the light of the subsequent 7/7 outrage in London. For the *maulid* which was celebrated with sacred song and chant and spiritual talks, offered those British Muslim youth an alternative to the grim choices of either a mindless secularism that alienates them from their very own souls, or the equally mindless and shallow but more immediately destructive radical fundamentalism or Islamism which empties Islam of its spiritual content and turns it into a radical, revolutionary ideology typical of the modern West but cast in the language of a formalized Islam.

Now what must be understood to appreciate this moment in a London suburb, at a mass gathering is that Shaykh Abu Bakr had always avoided an overtly public life and certainly anything resembling a mass gathering. That he chose this time, little more than a week before his death, to appear (and utterly inspire) the predominantly youthful audience of British Muslims is more than significant (and if the organizers had taken a much larger hall, there would have been an even bigger crowd to fill it, for all the tickets to this *Maulid* were gone within 48 hours of the announcement of the event). Could it be that the Shaykh (who deplored the politicization of Islam and the whole cult of development, which the Islamists in their own way subscribe to as much as their supposedly secularist opposites) sensed how desperate were the times and sought by personal presence to offer British Muslims a sense of a spiritual alternative?

This is of course a speculation, and I do not believe the Shaykh would have approved of my speculating upon the metahistorical significance of his person.

What matters is that Shaykh Abu Bakr simply said to the several thousand British Muslims gathered there: "The Prophet has not died, he is still with us, present with us, here and now."

And to that I add—Yes and with the Prophet, present with us, here and now, is our Shaykh, Abu Bakr Siraj al-Din.

S. Abdallah Schleifer
American University of Cairo
Cairo, Egypt

A TRIBUTE TO DR. MARTIN LINGS

Words could never suffice to pay tribute to my dear friend, Dr. Martin Lings, an honored colleague in matters related to William Shakespeare's works. Our interest in the spirituality of Shakespeare as reflected in his plays and sonnets was the link which brought Dr. Lings and me together initially.

After reading Dr. Lings' book on Shakespeare, I felt his contribution to Shakespeare scholarship was so remarkable that his thoughts should be recorded on film. In this filmed interview, Dr. Lings revealed much of the biographical history surrounding his interest and insight into Shakespeare. This began with his years at Oxford University where he studied under C.S. Lewis, and where he had his first transforming experience related to Shakespeare. Dr. Lings understood that Shakespeare's drama portrayed something of the beauty and harmony of the Creator's universal plan.

As Dr. Lings personal spiritual journey began in earnest, he was drawn to Egypt where the hand of Providence also enmeshed his life with William Shakespeare. During the 1940's and early 1950's, Dr. Lings lectured at Cairo University on Shakespeare and produced several plays.

This confluence of personal spiritual exploration and teaching of Shakespeare enabled Dr. Lings to perceive the esoteric meanings found in the esteemed poet's great works that eluded many erudite scholars. Dr. Lings had the full capacity to receive the wisdom of Shakespeare and to explain it clearly in his writing and lectures. Dr. Lings showed that Shakespeare was able to draw upon the transcendent and write upon which that which he knew and understood intellectually and spiritually. In reference to Shakespeare's works, Dr. Lings states: "truly inspired art is indeed a kind of white magic which casts a spell over man and momentarily changes him, doing as it were the impossible and making him quite literally excel himself."

As I stated earlier, my first acquaintance with Dr. Lings began through his interest in the esoteric aspects of Shakespeare's plays and mine in the spirituality found in the sonnets. What evolved from that, however, was quite remarkable. Dr. Martin Lings was of man of spiritual depth whose interest in people was not of the mundane. I perceived that he was a man of perfect truth and integrity who lived the life upon which his spiritual foundations were anchored. Through our conversations and correspondence, it was clear that Dr. Lings took a sincere interest in me as a person, but not in the ordinary way. Dr. Lings I knew thought of me, not just as a scholarly colleague, but as a child of God, a soul, as he was on the spiritual journey through life. Intuitively, I felt, that whatever he might have been able to do to lighten my journey, or enlighten my understanding overtly, or silently, he would do. His life, like Shakespeare's works, was "truly inspired art."

Dr. Martin Lings could draw upon the transcendent, and he had the capacity and interest in bringing others along with him on the golden pilgrimage of life. All of us are fortunate that such a man as Dr. Martin Lings has lived and given us an enduring legacy. I will miss his physical presence, but his life continues to touch mine in a very personal way.

> With Deepest Respect and Gratitude,
> Ira Zinman
> Encinitas, California

For Martin Lings

In the thirty years I knew Martin Lings he never changed. His preoccupation with the sacred, his clear exposition of the truth, his kindness, and his evident interiority were my first impressions of him and my last. Through thirty years of erratic and often halting growth on my part, and through my own times of difficulty and confusion, he remained a clear headed and confident friend and an impeccable spiritual advisor.

The last time I visited him at his home was about a year before his death. I had brought my wife to Westerham, in Kent, to meet him. We spoke of love. It was a topic he knew well. After a fascinating and helpful intellectual discussion, he told us stories of his own experiences and of what it had meant to him to have grown up in an atmosphere of love. He spoke of the warmth and closeness of his family and of his particular affection for his mother. It was a conversation we will never forget, not simply for the wealth of interesting and helpful information about the nature of love and its place in the Sufi path, but also for the unmistakable personal warmth that emanated from the Shaykh himself.

The other qualities that were so evident in the man were his precision and his integrity. All of these qualities he brought to the explication of the spiritual life, for his first love was the Sacred and thus the sacred pervaded everything he did and said. In every conversation I ever had with him it was manifest that he was constantly focused on the sacred and that this served as a touchstone for everything he said or did.

He was an artist whose keen visual sense, informed by his inner spiritual eye, transformed the world around him and the people in it. To this he brought a passion for the perfection these things deserved. Nowhere was this more obvious than in his garden where he created a scene that was both breathtakingly beautiful and magically interiorizing. This was an effort of many years and sometimes required many seasons to produce exactly the color he wanted in exactly the place he wanted it. His commitment to the things he loved was total. And so, too, all those who knew him understood that the meticulous care he gave to his garden was the same meticulous care he had given to his own soul and would give to the souls under his guidance.

His vision was also one of great depth which found its worthy object in the Quran and in Shakespeare. Everywhere he was able to show remarkable insight. His commentary on Shakespeare was unique and it revealed, without any doubt, the profoundly spiritual nature of Shakespeare's plays and their complex and elegant stories of the soul and the spirit. His own poetry and books combined his remarkable depth of insight with his acute visual sense; so his descriptions conveyed an almost palpable visual form and feeling, the result being not simply works of great depth and lucidity, but ones that brought abstruse things into clear light and showed them as knowable and as beautiful.

Clearly the Sacred deserves perfection, and this quality was evident in all he did. From the precision he gave his discussion of spiritual texts to the development of a particular color of flower for his garden. Nowhere was this more evident than in the care he gave the production of his last book on Quranic calligraphy which he held back from printing until the color plates were exactly as he thought they should be to convey the beauty of the original calligraphy.

His virtue was unmistakable in all he accomplished. His care of the sacred, the care he gave his wife as she became frail with age, and the gentle and precise care he gave to those who sought his spiritual guidance, all show the outward signs of inward depth and grace. As in all men of his stature, it was not simply that he knew the doctrine but that he practiced what he preached. I will miss him greatly. *Radiya' 'Llahu anhu*

Terry Moore
New York, New York

APPRECIATIONS FROM CAPE TOWN

Martin Lings, may God bless him and give him peace, was for us a veritable portrait of spiritual perfection, a mirror of what the *faqir* ought to become. His profound sense of the sacred, self-effacement, generosity of spirit, and a life dedicated to the remembrance of God made him a vehicle of a heavenly grace so rarely witnessed by men of our times. The *barakah* he radiated touched us deeply and above all aided us, in a very real way, in assimilating the essential truths of religion. His love of the sacred and all things sacred made us more attentive and sensitive to the manifestations of the sacred in its diverse forms. His embodiment of the spiritual virtues reflected with such clarity that it became for the *faqir* not only a yardstick wherewith to measure his own soul, but also an inducement to participate in such virtues. And when he spoke of Paradise he made it so real that it increased our desire and longing for it. May God give him a place in the highest regions of *firdaus*.

'Alawi, Yasminah, and friends
Cape Town, South Africa

If, as we have been told, the modern world has created an environment in which "the very existence of God seems improbable," then surely Heaven itself must feel the need to supply the remedy to this. Two of the most effective means of reminding men of "the one thing needful," I have found, is the teacher of spiritual science (theology in the broadest sense), and the witness "in the flesh." It is particularly this second type of "witness" (without, of course, excluding the first) that I have come to identify with the late Dr. Martin Lings.

From my very first meeting with him in 1984, until his last visit to his friends here in Cape Town in February of 2005, Dr. Lings has always struck me as a man whom God has blessed with the singular gift of being able to make concrete the presence of "the Motionless Mover." Whether it be on a walk in nature, or at a dinner, his native reflex was always to remind one of Heaven and what it was that pleased Heaven most; and to do this in a "personal style" saturated with beauty and generosity: a master of the art of the "action of presence." And in all of this, profoundest thanks are of course also due to his wife, Mrs. Lesley Lings, who so wonderfully mirrors her husband's vocation. *Ad majorem Dei gloriam.*

Grateful admirer
Cape Town, South Africa

"Seek ye first the kingdom of God … and all these things (of the world) shall be added unto thee": the life of Dr. Martin Lings was an outstanding and memorable application of this spiritual injunction of Christ. For him the spiritual counted first of all; the world would order itself—or rather, God would order it for him—in due course. "Whoso protecteth God in his heart, him will God protect in the world," said the Prophet of Islam; it was one of the many eminences of Dr. Lings, and of his beloved widow Mrs. Lings, to know and live this with all his heart. May God bless his soul, and bless us through him.

Clinton Minnaar
Cape Town, South Africa

I met him only once, when he generously agreed to see me in his beautiful cottage. This meeting left a lasting impression on me. Another time, I wrote to him to ask what he thought of dating the oldest available Quranic manuscripts using modern archeological methods. He later kindly wrote me a letter in his own handwriting and offered his opinion. I still keep this letter in my copy of *The Quranic Art of Calligraphy and Illumination*, and eagerly await the new edition, perfected as he wanted it to be.

Dr. Riaz Uddin Riaz
Osmania University
Hyderabad, India

Martin Lings

He explained the religion of Islam in his books and in his talks in such a clear and quiet manner. His ecumenism and all-inclusive beliefs gave me a feeling of profound peace, a peace which I felt was his personal essence.

Elsa Rennes Bogary
Gstaad, Switzerland

On Martin Lings

Martin Lings seems to me a man profoundly quiet. He was accomplished and honored; he had much to teach but nothing to prove. In his writings, which I have read fairly extensively, he neither condescends to the reader nor appeals for the reader's indulgence, but says merely and plainly what he knows. His aim, as he put it, was to make his work "reliable in that it is not written any more simply then the truth allows." I am particularly indebted to him for his book on Shakespeare, which I think of and return to again and again.

Wendell Berry, poet and author
Port Royal, Kentucky

ON SHAYKH ABU BAKR

The first characteristic that comes to my mind when thinking of Sidi Abu Bakr is: utter faithfulness to his spiritual master, Shaykh Aissa, (Jesus in Arabic). From Egypt where he had been living, he would come every summer to Switzerland for a whole month in order to see the Shaykh as often as possible. We would go for long walks with his wife, Sayyidah Rabia, either in the mountains or by the lake of Geneva, during which the two men would have conversations on all possible subjects, interrupted only by moments of contemplating the beauties of nature, the flowers, the streams, the snow-covered Alps...

Sidi Abu Bakr was most eager to absorb the wise teachings of his Master, as an empty vessel ready to be filled. And thus, over the years, he grew into a saintly master himself, who was able to pour the drink he had so eagerly absorbed to the many disciples he used to faithfully visit, year after year, all over the world.

Catherine Schuon
Bloomington, Indiana

ON SAYYIDA RABIA'

Homage should be rendered to Sayyida Rabia', née Lesley Smalley, widow of Dr. Martin Lings. This noble lady continues to be a model of spiritual fortitude in her own right. Always the bulwark in the shadow of Shaykh Abu Bakr (Dr. Lings), she lived her own inner life, whilst at the same time selflessly welcoming and serving the continual flow of disciples and spiritual seekers who regularly frequented their home. She is completely humble and self-effaced, yet her dry wit and pearls of wisdom will always be unforgettable. During the time of her physical disability, Shaykh Abu Bakr (Dr. Lings) served her faithfully at home, and continued to do so until his final day. Indeed they were a couple who modeled a relationship based on the highest spiritual values.

Jane Fatima Casewit
Rabat, Morocco

Memories of Dr. Martin Lings

My first encounter with Dr. Martin Lings was in 1978. I had been invited to his fairy-tale house for a traditional gathering that included a walk in the enchanted fields and woodlands nearby. Normally, each guest would have his turn conversing with him and trying to keep up with his sprightly stride. On this occasion, he was having some problems with his voice. When he motioned to me to stroll beside him, he said in almost a whisper, "I am sorry, I won't be able to talk much as my doctor has ordered me to minimize speaking." Looking around me at the deep green foliage, I responded, "Nature will be articulate in your stead." Our eyes met briefly, and I saw that he was pleased with my response.

A year or two later, we met again, this time in the Kingdom of Morocco. My wife and I had the honor of fetching him at the airport of Casablanca and driving him down to Marrakesh and the foothills of the High Atlas Mountains. En route, our vehicle had a flat tire. We pulled to the side of the road and got out. Looking down at the punctured tire with an air of detached bewilderment, he apologized for not being able to assist me, saying that he knew nothing about automobiles (he had never learned to drive). I suggested that they wait in the shade of some nearby Eucalyptus trees, while I changed it. When I had finished, my hands still grimy, I went over to inform him that we could continue our trip. Standing there serenely, a simple Egyptian-style cape thrown over his shoulders and a felt cap on his head, he exuded the aura of a medieval sage who had somehow been transplanted into our dissipated, dysfunctional world of machines. He was at once aloof, majestic and child-like, grateful for small things.

It was in Mecca, in 1987, while performing the lesser pilgrimage, that I felt the most powerful sentiments of filial piety for Dr. Lings. Despite a debilitating pain in one of his legs, he had completed the physically demanding rituals of the *'Umrah*. We were sitting next to each other in the marble court facing the *Ka'bah* waiting for the call for the sunset prayer. Throngs of pilgrims circulated around us and several times I sought to protect his diminutive figure from careless feet. At one point, I had to firmly redirect the misstep of a fellow Muslim, who turned to me and said in Arabic, "Take good care of your father." Speechless for a moment, I then replied, "I wish he were my father!" I don't think Dr. Lings overheard our exchange, for he was immersed in the remembrance of his Lord.

May God be well pleased with al-Hājj Abū Bakr Sirāj ad-Dīn, and have mercy on all those who regard themselves as his children. Amen.

Stephen Daoud Casewit
Rabat, Morocco

A MESSAGE OF HOPE AT THE ELEVENTH HOUR
MARTIN LINGS, 1909-2005
BY HIS NEIGHBOUR AND DISCIPLE

'The Spirit bloweth where it listeth and thou hearest the sound thereof, but canst not tell whence it cometh, and whither it goeth. So is every one that is born of the Spirit."

John 3:8

A few days before he died Martin Lings put the finishing touches to his last book, fittingly entitled *A Return to the Spirit*. A man who had indeed been "born of the Spirit" was now declaring his readiness to return thereto, having lived his entire life in utter dedication to it. The book is indeed his valedictory message. It offers, as the subtitle of the book promises (*Questions and Answers*), a series of answers to some of the most funda-

149

mental questions being posed by seekers today; answers which are profound and yet at the same time disarmingly simple—this combination of profundity and simplicity having always characterized his style of doctrinal exposition.

There is no question more fundamental or simple than that with which the book begins: how does one put first things first, and it is entirely appropriate that this opening chapter is dedicated to the influence upon him of Frithjof Schuon, who, more than anyone else, helped him put first things first. Anyone wishing to know who Martin Lings was would have to begin by understanding his complete and immutable devotion to his teacher. To praise Lings is, inescapably, to praise Schuon, just as one cannot praise a painting without praising its painter; Lings was the very embodiment of the essential teachings of Schuon. The "painting" however, went on to become a painter in its turn, and while always maintaining unimpeachable fidelity to his teacher's guidance, imparted to that guidance the accent, fragrance or colour of his own personality, in accordance with the maxim of Junayd: "Water takes on the colour of the cup." Thus, in the personality and the writings of Martin Lings we see not just a fruit of the way inaugurated by Frithjof Schuon but also a particularly striking mode of holiness bearing the unique stamp of his own distinctive personality. The man was—according to most of those who knew him intimately—a saint, in Islamic terms, a "friend of God" (*walī Allāh*). If Islam had anything akin to a formal procedure for canonisation, such a procedure would undoubtedly have begun immediately upon the passing away of this great soul, known in the Muslim world as Shaykh Abu Bakr Siraj ad-Din. In the Islamic tradition, however, saints are not canonised after death, they are recognised in their lifetime. The number of people who expressed their conviction that this man was indeed a saint is remarkable and can be taken as an expression of the principle *vox populi vox Dei.*

At the end of his life, Martin Lings radiated the holy fragrance of one who had lived his entire life dedicated to the "one thing needful"; the *baraka* of nearly seven decades of faithful, sincere, fervent invocation of the Divine Name was evident to all those who were privileged to come into contact with him. He was someone who knew that the best of acts was the invocation of the Name of God; in his presence the radiance of this best of acts could be felt in an almost tangible manner. The Qur'an tells us that *A good word is as a good tree: its root is firm, its branches are in heaven* (XIV, 24), to which Martin Lings adds this crucial comment: "This may be interpreted: an invocation, and above all the Supreme Name which is the best of good words, is not a flat utterance which spreads horizontally outwards in this world to be lost in thin air, but a vertical continuity of repercussions throughout all the states of being." For Martin Lings this perception of the sacramental efficacy of the invocation was not merely theoretical; what he describes is what he experienced, and what we could not help but sense: the divine Name truly "re-verberated" throughout his being, and a being penetrated by the Name is a being penetrated by the Named, a sanctified being, for, as it is said in Sufism: *al-ism huwa'l-musammā*, the Name is the Named.

If sanctification herebelow be "proof" of salvation hereafter, the presence of this man was irrefutable proof that the remembrance of God is not just a practice confined to a particular time and place, but a permanently flowing fountain of grace that can truly come to determine the whole of one's life, and even overflow into the lives of others. The "friends of God"— the "slaves" as opposed to the "righteous"—are those whose very hearts have become one with the fountain of remembrance from which they drink, and in drinking from it, they increase the flow of the fountain. It is to this mystery of radiant realization that the following verses of the Qur'an allude: *Truly the righteous shall drink from a filled cup* [containing a drink] *flavoured with Kāfūr—A fountain from which the slaves of God drink, making it flow with greater abundance* (LXXIV: 5–6). To be in this man's presence was truly to drink at the fountain of the remembrance of God.

When one thinks of the character of Martin Lings many qualities come to mind—humility, generosity, discipline, fidelity, wisdom. But one quality which strikes us as particularly apt in summing up his personality is expressed by the Arabic word *lutf*, which cannot be translated into English by a single word. It expresses a synthesis of the qualities of grace and compassion, loving-kindness and gentleness, intelligence and subtlety, but also, given its divine archetype, it denotes a certain power. "Al-Latīf," one of the most potent of all the divine Names, expresses, in addition to the gentle qualities, that irresistible force which surges forth from the intangible depths of infinite subtlety. It is for this reason that one has recourse to the invocation, "Yā Latīf" only in times of direst need. Now Martin Lings was truly *latīf* in all these senses—his gentle, kind disposition was but the surface expression of a strong character implacably rooted in the Absolute, a character which radiated through great subtlety of intelligence and a flawless aesthetic sensibility. To encounter this combination of radiant generosity and adamantine discipline, penetrating intelligence and purity of soul, was to experience nothing less than the attraction of divine grace, of *lutf*, gentle and sweet, yet of immense power. This same quality can be sensed in his writings—unshakeable certitude and intellectual authority are expressed with a lightness of touch, an elegant simplicity; his style of writing was as attractive as its content was convincing.

Martin Lings was indeed a master of the English language, as all his books demonstrate, but nowhere is this mastery more clearly revealed than in his poems, each of which, we dare say, is a masterpiece. As his early teacher at Oxford, C.S. Lewis exclaimed, upon receiving the poems: "This is true poetry!" It is only a question of time before he is recognised as the great poet that he was. We shall return to his poems shortly. But mentioning "time" brings us to the question of Martin Lings' attitude to the age in which we live. In common with the other great exponents of the perennial philosophy he of course viewed this age as one of decadence and decline; at this "eleventh hour," one can expect nothing but further degeneration, in global terms, and despite inevitable fluctuations in particular domains, until the end of this cycle.

However, from a more fundamental—indeed, properly "perennial"—point of view, the life and works of Martin Lings, are testimony to the immensely positive potential for spirituality that is present in our times; a potential, indeed, which can never be discounted, for "the Spirit bloweth where it listeth." There is no place here for pessimism: *for who despairs of the mercy of his Lord except those who stray?*, as the Qur'an asks rhetorically (XV: 56). On the contrary, Martin Lings delivered to us all a message of hope, of spiritual hope, that is, a hope which already participates in the object hoped-for. For the eleventh hour is characterised not only by darkness, but also by divine mercy, glimmerings of light which are all the more conspicuous against the background of the prevailing gloom: it is upon this aspect of mercy and grace, compensating for the global decadence, that Martin Lings was fixated, and not on the decadence itself. The parable of the eleventh hour given by Jesus—the fact that the workers who worked only for the eleventh hour received the same wage as those who worked throughout the heat of the day—clearly refers to the "increase" of mercy at the end of time, a principle affirmed in Islam by the saying of the Prophet: "He who omits one tenth of the Law in the beginning of Islam will be damned; but he who accomplishes one tenth of the Law at the end of Islam will be saved." Divine mercy super-abundantly compensates for human decadence. "Truly, My Mercy takes precedence over My Wrath," according to a *hadīth qudsī*; *My mercy encompasses all things*, according to the Qur'an (VII: 156).

The darkness of our times, of the imminence of the end of the cycle, was indeed stressed by Martin Lings in his books and discourse, but not in order to inculcate a sense of doom and gloom; rather, in order to precipitate our awareness of the need to take advantage of the immense compensations of divine grace: every moment, he used to say often, is to be transformed into a "moment of mercy." One should avail oneself, in every single moment, of all the "available" mercy, and thus galvanise one's soul for "the one thing needful."

The present age, moreover, assists the spiritual seeker indirectly, through the very "momentum" generated by its frenetic activity as it approaches its final throes; the very "pull" of the Hour can be harnessed to spiritual aspiration, even after one has passed from the "market" (remaining passive in outward profanity) to the "vineyard" (activity with regard to the Kingdom of Heaven): "… the liberating efforts of intelligence and will that are thus called into action may be prolonged, after the vineyard has been reached, to add their momentum, combined with that of the eleventh hour itself, to the 'work,' that is, to the spiritual path."

As he often used to say, "Mercy will have the last word." We who were privileged to receive the guidance of this great soul were given two types of "proof" of this mercy, the one principle and objective, deriving from awareness of the doctrines, both metaphysical and cosmological, teaching us that mercy, beauty, and beatitude pertain to the essence of the Real, and that mercy compensates for the increasing decadence of the "last days." The other "proof" was personal and existential: that is, the very soul of Martin Lings itself was indubitable proof of the "availability" of mercy even in these dark times, a sign that the "Spirit bloweth where it listeth," concrete evidence that the ultimate goal is still accessible even in our most adverse conditions, a demonstration "in the flesh" that the perennial wisdom is truly perennial, both in principle *and* practice, and thus cannot be eclipsed by any passing clouds of modernist misosophy or materialistic "culture," however dark they may be.

This was Martin Lings' greatest gift to his disciples and students all over the world: he not only expressed by his eloquent words, but manifested by his sanctified being, a message of hope, a spiritual "optimism," rooted in aspiration for the only goal that is ever worth pursuing, whatever the age or era. He not only proved existentially, beyond all need for logical demonstration, that the highest ideals are still realizable: the radiance of his *lutf* rendered these ideals attractive and powerful and utterly irresistible.

To return to his poetry, the poem entitled "Self-Portrait" expresses well the joy that emanates from a soul imbued with the perennial spirit, even though born in such an anti-traditional age; it shows beautifully that the perennialist is not a sentimental traditionalist, bemoaning our times and wishing he were born in some pre-modern age. After referring to various revela-

tions, and apparently sorrowing at his absence at these marvellous moments when Heaven touched earth directly, he finally
expresses his absence from the *bay'at a-ridwān*, "the pact of
[divine] beatitude," when the believers made the pact of allegiance to the Prophet "beneath the tree," the prototype of the
esoteric initiation in Islam; and then concludes with the real
meaning of his "lament":

> When half a thousand years and more
> Had passed, and men allegiance swore
> To the Arab Prophet, beneath the tree,
> My willing hand was still not free
> From bonds of time and space to be
> Between his hands in fealty.
>
> Such blessings missed, time was when I
> Within myself would wonder why,
> Half quarrelling with the book of fate
> For having writ me down so late.
> But now I no longer my lot
> Can question, and of what was not.
> No more I say: Would it had been!
> For I have seen what I have seen,
> And I have heard what I have heard.
> So if to tears ye see me stirred,
> Presume not that they spring from woe:
> In thankful wonderment they flow.
> Praise be to Him, the Lord, the King,
> Who gives beyond all reckoning.

This poem expresses what everybody in our times can "see"
and "hear" if we but open our eyes and ears: the marvellous,
diverse manifestations of the Logos, whose essence is beyond
time and space, and thus accessible always and everywhere.
"Before Abraham was, I am," said Jesus, expressing his nature
as the Logos; it is to this timeless Logos that the *haqīqa
muhammadiyya* likewise refers: "I was a Prophet when Adam
was still between water and clay." Instead of dwelling on the

negative features of our times, Martin Lings urged us to take advantage of the "wisdom" that also accompanies the "old age" of the cosmos, reminding us that terminality rejoins primordiality. This wisdom is nothing less than the spiritual patrimony of mankind—of all mankind and not any one particular religious sector. In this patrimony we can truly rejoice, shed tears of wonderment, and receive that spiritual sustenance (*rizq*) to which the last line of the poem alludes. We are sure that the poet wished us to recall here the words uttered by the Blessed Virgin, when asked by Zakariyya from whence she had received the *rizq* that he found with her, miraculously, for the *rizq* in question was, according to tradition, "fruits out of season." These words come in a verse of the Qur'an especially dear to Martin Lings, for many reasons. The Blessed Virgin replies to Zakariyya: *It is from God; verily God giveth sustenance to whom He will beyond all reckoning* (III: 37). (*Huwa min 'indi'Llāh; inna'Llāha yarzuqu man yashā'u bi-ghayri-hisāb*)

To return to the image of the good word as a good tree, let us recall that the verse of the Qur'an continues with an image that we can apply to perennial wisdom itself: a "fruit" that is always accessible, one which is brought into harmonious reverberation with our deepest being by the best of acts, the invocation of the Name of God: *A good word is as a good tree: its root is firm, its branches are in heaven. It giveth forth its fruits at all times, by the permission of its Lord ...* (XIV, 24–25).

Two days before he died, Martin Lings planted a tree, a liburnam. He thus symbolically re-enacted that for the sake of which he lived all his life—planting the seed of the remembrance in his own heart, and in the hearts of all those who were blessed by his guidance. This is also what the Prophet of Islam bade us do: "When you see the Hour approaching, plant a tree."

*****

We can fittingly conclude this homage to our teacher by quoting what he wrote himself in respect of the "archetype of devotional homage," He is clearly describing what he experienced upon coming into "contact with actual perfection"; but he also, and entirely unwittingly, describes accurately what many of us, as his disciples, experienced in regard to our own contact with him:

" … all devotional homage, all hero-worship worthy of the name, proceeds subjectively from the perfection which exists in every soul, even though, in the majority, it has been buried under the rubble of a fallen second nature. If the burial is too deep, the sense of values can be irremediably vitiated; but even a remote consciousness of the latent perfection is enough to serve as a basis for having ideals and to arouse in souls, at contact with actual perfection, the nostalgic recognition of a fulfilment which for themselves is also a possibility and a goal to be reached."

That, precisely, is the message of hope given and embodied by Martin Lings at the "eleventh hour": he helped to arouse within us the "nostalgic recognition of a fulfilment," the ultimate fulfilment, which is for us also a "possibility and a goal to be reached."

May God be well-pleased with him and sanctify his mystery.

Radiya'Llāhu 'anhu wa qaddasa sirrahu.

> Reza Shah-Kazemi
> Westerham, Kent, United Kingdom
> Reprinted from *The Sacred Web*,
> vol. 15, 2005

A RICH GIVER

Martin Lings was an inestimable treasure living amongst us. He was like no other Englishman. For me Martin Lings *was* England. He was its sky and clouds, its green fields and trees, its rain. To those who loved him—and they were not few—he was our "Spring Summer"; he was "abundance that seems endless and forever." (See "Martin Lings: Collected Poems" winter 1999 issue of *Sophia* [volume 5, number 2] dedicated to him on the occasion of his 90th birthday.)

In January 1990 I went on a trip to Egypt with my mother, sister, future brother-in-law, and another friend. Having spent a year in Cairo as part of my Arabic studies at Oxford University I felt I could show them the best of Egypt. At the end of the journey I stayed behind in Cairo to visit friends. One of the friends I went to visit was Julian Johansen and his wife, Alison. Julian had become a Muslim during our undergraduate days at Oxford and had taken the name Abd ar-Rahman. We would occasionally talk about Islam together and I remember telling him, "I can say '*La ilaha illa 'Llah* (there is no divinity other than God)' but I doubt I could ever say with conviction, '*Muhammadun rasulu 'Llah* (Muhammad is His messenger).'"

The Johansens had an English neighbor by the name of Abd al-Azim who had entered a Sufi order and was having certain difficulties. Abd al-Rahman suggested that he might benefit from meeting Dr. Martin Lings, who was visiting Cairo at that time. A meeting was arranged and I went along as the chauffer.

When he opened the door of his hotel room, I, for the first time, beheld Martin Lings. His beautiful and dignified face was framed by his straight hair and fine beard. Despite his advanced years his every movement was nimble. Above all I was struck by the lovely quality of his measured voice as he welcomed us in.

Feeling that I may be intruding, I made to absent myself, but Lings immediately said that I should stay and engaged me in a short conversation. He asked me what I was doing in Cairo. I mentioned that I had recently returned from Luxor. I happened to add that I had visited Gurna Gedida, a small village built by the architect Hassan Fathy using traditional adobe building techniques. His face lit up and he informed me that he had known Hassan Fathy; that they had made the pilgrimage to Mecca together. Following this short exchange I withdrew to the side of the room and sat looking out over the Nile. We all fell into a peaceful, and pleasant silence, waiting for Abd al-Azim to formulate his question. After a while, and by way of helping Abd al-Azim break the ice, Lings asked, "Is there anything you'd like to ask me?"

I can hear the sound of his voice even now, a decade and a half later. His words, which were ostensibly directed at Abd al-Azim, in an instant wrenched me out of my tranquil calm and plunged me into a sudden and intense alertness. His voice entered my being like a powerful wave and gathered and pressed around my heart. From his first utterance I entered into a state, the like of which I doubt I will ever experience again. Had I been standing, I would certainly have fallen to the ground. I thought to turn around to see if anyone in the room had been disturbed by the sound of my racing heart.

I cannot really put into words or even clearly recall what happened to me in those few moments, but I do recall a chain of thoughts in the form of an argument, which ran something as follows:

> You have for long been certain of the reality of God. Existence itself substantiates that. How can even the empty void, into which things are placed, "be" without the tremendous miracle of some Power one must call God? You always used to argue that religions are just well-intentioned, man-made constructs. But you forget one thing—if existence is a proof for God, do not forget that you yourself are also something existent, and that the great Bringer-into-being of existence determined you also, with your consciousness which recognizes the self-evident-ness of God and is calling out to know more about Him. Would not this God, who has given you existence and consciousness, not also have provided you with the content for which that consciousness is searching? Clearly, God would not bring into existence this consciousness without giving it the content it required. Every conscious mind that has ever existed must have had access to this content. Now, I have not experienced receiving such a content directly. I must therefore look for it in my immediate environment. (What I later heard from Lings did not occur to me at this time, namely, that the first revelation of all is Nature itself, whose signs we are no longer able to read clearly.) Certain individuals must have received this content in order that I may have access to it. These individuals must be the prophets; this content must be the religions. Yes, it's as simple as that: religions must all come from God, each an essential message sufficient for our needs.

There must be many religions. Each community of men that has ever existed must have had a religion.

Now, the man before me speaks as a Muslim. Islam must be one of these messages from God. So—I agree; there is no divinity other than God, and Muhammad is clearly His messenger. Had Lings been a Buddhist, I would probably have become a Buddhist. What I knew was that the man whose voice had penetrated to the core of my being was a Muslim, and if Islam leads to this supreme human possibility, then I would follow this way.

What I did not realize until later is that I had—as if by osmosis—absorbed the key tenet of Martin Lings' belief in the universal equality of all Heaven-sent religions. This universalist credo is explicitly expressed in the Qur'an itself as a belief in 'Allah and His angels, His books and His messengers: *We make no distinction between any of His messengers* (II, 258). The Qur'an likewise in several places informs us that each people has been sent a messenger and has received a guidance (see X, 47 for example). Particularly significant in this regard is the verse (V, 69—see also the almost identical II, 62 and compare II, 38):

> Verily the faithful, and the Jews, and the Sabeans, and the Christians—whoso believeth in God and the Last Day and doeth deeds of piety, no fear shall come upon them neither shall they grieve.

One meets Muslims who would deny the validity of Judaism and Christianity. They would dismiss verses such as these claiming that they would have been abrogated by later Qur'anic verses. Martin Lings, who always had just the right argument for things, would point out that the last revealed section of the Qur'an, which clearly cannot be subject to abrogation, shows that "God accepts the sacrifice of the Jews" whose food it makes licit for Muslims. Clearly Judaism, and by extension the other religions, remain valid.

On several occasions in recent years I heard Lings say, words like, "The average Muslim is prepared to sacrifice the glory of

God five times a day to the glory of Islam. Now, the Qur'an states that, *They have not rated God at His true worth—la qaddaru 'Llaha haqqa qadrih*. Our *Tariqah* tries to avoid that criticism as far as is humanly possible—of course, only God can rate Himself at His own true worth."

As a young man, Lings prayed that in the Autumn of his life he might become a "rich giver" (The South Wind, *Collected Poems*, Archetype 2002). I was one of the many recipients of that compassionate prayer. Through him I received my religion and my spiritual way. He was as a father to me, and like so many of his children, I loved and continue to love him dearly.

Martin Lings' very presence was transforming. In his company one was raised above oneself; one became something of that which one ought to be. Titus Burkhardt—in writing about sacred art—said that, "it makes men participate naturally and almost involuntarily in the world of holiness." These words describe perfectly what it was to be with Martin Lings. In *Splendours of Qur'an Calligraphy and Illumination* (Thesaurus Islamicus Foundation, pre-publication edition, p.17), Lings says the following:

> The Qur'an makes it clear that a Prophet must be considered as a Divine masterpiece. In one passage, God says to Moses what could be translated: *I have fashioned thee as a work of art for Myself* (XX, 41), and in another, Muhammad is told: *Verily of an immense magnitude is thy nature* (LXVIII, 4).

Martin Lings—*Mawlana*, Shaykh Abu Bakr Siraj ad-Din—was a saint living amongst us. He was a work of sacred art; a Heaven-sent masterpiece. I thank Heaven for this incomparable gift, and I pray for his spirit's delight in Paradise and for his delight in the meeting with his Lord.

Justin Majzub
Oxford, England

Life is a Gradual Demonstration

When I considered recording a few personal recollections of my years with Martin Lings, I found myself daunted by this— in no way up to putting my heart's experience into words. I first met him at the British Museum in 1976 when I brought students from Cairo to attend the World of Islam Festival in London. What I thought was to be a cup of tea and a discussion regarding collaboration on a small video presenting Islam through its great art, architecture and calligraphy became the turning point in my life when we concluded and he quietly counseled, "You must *do* something about your*self*." My aim for life had always been the process of sanctification—but for the most part my efforts had been "outer." Here for the first time in my life I encountered a person of the West (from my own culture) who clearly was egoless. Anyone knows from a study of religion that such humility is the basis of sacred living and is, in itself, the greatest service for therein is God's presence. The Ocean can only pour in when one goes below sea level—and here it was before me—a realized example of this possibility. And so began nearly thirty years of my heart's attempt to imitate his way of being—to be that kind of loving, utterly generous presence that Divine Destiny had brought mercifully into my days. Never had I met a person so transparent—or translucent, so empty of all but God.

In the years that followed our family was blessed to have him regularly stay in our home—for more than a decade in Cambridge and the surrounding villages where we lived, learned, and published and then ever since, for a few weeks each winter in our Cairo homes. I mostly think of the quiet breakfasts—or lunches where all he wanted to eat was a small cup of lentil soup. One never knew when the next thing he might say would transport the soul to a new level of understanding and resolve. Once he was telling us about the time in Cairo when Sayidayy Nafisa, one of the great grand-daughters of the Prophet—peace be upon him—was approached by crowds of people who were greatly suffering from drought—the Nile was devastatingly low. Tears rolled down Shaykh Abu Bakr's cheeks as he related that when Sayida Nafisa went to the river's banks and tossed in her head scarf, instantly the waters rose.

On another occasion over breakfast we spoke of his book, *Symbol and Archetype: A Study of the Meaning of Existence.* When I mentioned it was in many ways my favorite of his works he said it was for him as well. In my own volume of this work, next to the inscription he wrote for me on that 1994 Cairo morning, I noted, " …We spoke much of Paradise—of purified souls and the last *umra* for us both." On other mornings we returned to the death of his mother, who had also entered Islam. We used to weep together when he described her luminous body after her long struggle with a dreadful illness.

When I think of visiting his home in Kent, and the wonderful walks in the surrounding countryside and woods, I recall that on a particular Sunday afternoon as we were returning and headed towards his own garden's gate, birds joyously flew out to greet and welcome him home. When he knelt gardening these creatures of the sky kept close company with him—often sitting on his trowel plunged beside him in the earth. Besides these winged companions, a wild peacock adopted the Lings, and often pranced conspicuously back and forth on the roof top of the place of prayer. But now Shaykh Abu Bakr has returned from the sublime garden he tended to The Garden of Paradise and to the Gardener.

I always feared the day his presence would be taken from me—when my eyes could no longer behold him as he sat silently in prayer and remembrance of God—when my ears could no longer hear him walking all the night in his bedroom, invoking the Name of God—groaning with longing for Union. But I have found he is not absent.

Al-Ghazali (d. 1111 C.E.) commented that man has three basic human needs—first food, then clothing, and finally shelter—and that mankind in the over-refinement and concern for these needs, has forgotten both his Beginning and End. I never knew anyone who ate, dressed, and lived as simply and humbly as Shaykh Abu Bakr, whose entire focus was on our True Origin and Return to the Spirit.

In his *Lata'if al-Minan*, or *Subtle Blessings*, Ibn 'Ata' Al-lah al-Iskandari (d. 1303 C.E.) says, "Know—may God have mercy on you—that the abstinence of the elect is understood by few ... it includes their vigilance against being enticed by this world or diverted by the life to come (from seeking God Himself). They are wary of this life out of loyalty (to God), and of the life to come out of the desire to be devoted purely to God alone." And this can be further understood from the mentioning of al-Ghazali, that "Each thing hath two faces, a face of its own and a face of its Lord; in respect of its own face it is nothingness, and in respect of the face of God it is Being. Thus there is nothing in existence save only God and His Face, for everything perisheth but His Face always and forever."

In 1995 Sidi Abu Bakr was lecturing on Shakespeare at a congress on sacred art in Tehran, where I delivered a paper on the symbolism of the cherubim—on the duality that guards the way to the Tree of Life. A few weeks earlier I had been extremely ill with heart problems and in a few hours of surrender experienced the Oneness of God's Infinite, Luminous Presence – in which nothing else exists. I explained to Sidi Abu Bakr that I didn't *deserve* this grace. He said, "Is anyone worthy of the blessings that come? No. Does anyone deserve the trials? No. Because they are the *same thing*—there is no duality— only God *adjusting* us to the Center."

I conclude with my favorite lines, presented many years ago to me by my son, from al-Junayd of the ninth century C.E.

> The Saint hath no fear,
> because fear is the expectation
> either of some future calamity
> or of the eventual loss of some object of desire;
> whereas the Saint is the "son of his time"
> (and resides in the Eternal Presence/Present);
> he has no future from which he should fear anything
> and, as he hath no fear,
> so he hath no hope
> since hope is the expectation either of gaining an
> object of desire

or being relieved from a misfortune,
and this belongs to the future;
nor does he grieve
because grief arises from the rigor of time,
and how should he feel grief
who dwells in the Radiance of Satisfaction
and the Garden of Concord.

Virginia Gray Henry-Blakemore
Louisville, Kentucky

Shaykh Abu Bakr Siraj al-Din was the love of my life. There are no more books to read. It remains only to follow what he said. I knew him since the age of six and when we gathered to pray with him we entered Paradise. While my heart is truly sad to be separated from him I have the ultimate consolation: Paradise is now in the Name.

MG
Merida, Venezuela

As Shaykh Abu Bakr was leaving Cairo for what would be the last time, tears welled up in my eyes as they always did when this most beloved and saintly man would leave us. It was as if something was being wrenched from our hearts every time we said good-bye. I approached Shaykh Abu Bakr and said, "Mawlana, we love you dearly". He replied, "And I love you dearly". I shall live the rest of my days on these words and try to be the very thing that he loved. Shaykh Abu Bakr was victorious over life and death; to have been blessed with his excellent example was the greatest gift in the world. There are really no words to describe how those who knew and loved him will miss him.

Haajar Gouverneur
Cairo, Egypt

Martin Lings

AN AID TO CONCENTRATION ON THE WORDS
AND THE MOVEMENTS OF THE CANONICAL PRAYER *AS-SALAH*

A TALK BY MARTIN LINGS
JANUARY, 2005
CAIRO, EGYPT

In the *takbir,* which opens the *salah,* the hand placed on the ear is a ritual enactment of the words *'we hear and obey'* which follow the Qur'anic credo (II, 287). The hand here symbolizes the free will, which man alone of all earthly creatures possesses and which makes him alone capable of deliberate obedience, unlike the animals which are bound to follow their instincts.

The words of the *takbir*, without the gesture, are repeated throughout the *salah* at every moment except one which, as we shall see, expresses another blessed reality which must not be lost sight of.

The *Hamdalah* with which the Qur'anic text of the *salah* opens (an introductory *basmalah* is permissible but not obligatory) imposes on the soul a mood of intense gratitude, for 'One praises God not only because He is the Sovereign Good but also because He has given us birth at the Gate of Paradise.' We alone, of all earthly creatures, are endowed with faculties which enable us, if we take advantage of them, to pass through that Gate. Our gratitude is prolonged by the Names of Mercy which follow the *Hamdalah,* and by the reminder that it is the All-Merciful who is *the Owner of the Day of Judgement.* In other words it is He who makes all final decisions which concern our ultimate ends.

The words *Thee we worship and from Thee we seek help* bring us to the supplication itself: *Guide us upon the way of Transcendence, the way of those on whom Thy Grace is, not those who deserve anger nor those who are astray.*

In the obeisance (*ruku*) which follows our recitation from the Qur'an we glorify three times the Almighty, *al-Azim.* We rise from the *ruku* with the words 'God hearkeneth unto whoso praiseth Him', which recall His Qur'anic Self-description: *I answer the prayer of the pray-er when he prayeth Me* (II, 186). His answering of our prayer to be able to transcend our earthly state qualifies us for the rite of prostration (*sujud*). In this connection we must remember that the Prophet said: 'The slave is nearest unto his Lord when he is prostrate.' He also said: 'I was granted coolness of the eyes in the *salah*', that is, he was made to delight in it. The three glorifications of the All-Highest which coincide with nearestness must therefore be joyous. For the first, let us remember that the human initiative of discernment is transformed by the Divine Presence into illumination; for the second glorification let us have in mind the Sovereign Good, that is, the Absolute Infinite Perfection of God, and for the third, the truth that this Goodness is the Sole Reality.

The sitting position (*julus*) which immediately follows the first prostration is a backward movement which takes us from objectivity to subjectivity. The object is always in front whereas the subject is always behind. Our consciousness of being 'I' can be located somewhere in the region of the heart. The vocation of man is to attach himself to the Real ... the Great Peace. For the three glorifications of the second prostration, let us therefore dwell on this ultimate blessing with an increasing intensity of gladness.

The *julus* which follows this prostration is, when it occurs in the second or in the final *rak'ah*, the first repose which the body has been allowed since the beginning of the *salah*. Let this relaxation be identified with the Peace of our finality, that Peace being the central theme of the *tahiyyah* (greeting) which is now uttered while we remain seated.

The Qur'an has promised two Paradises to each soul that is saved. It is in the lower of these that the communion of Saints takes place. The higher Paradise is our meeting with God. These twofold blessings are the theme of the final verses of the Surat al-Fajr (LXXXIX, 27–30):

O thou soul which art at peace, return unto thy Lord in gladness that is thine in Him and His in thee. Enter thou among My slaves; enter thou My Paradise.

From now on the human plane has been transcended: the soul's supplication has been transformed into the Spirit's affirmation of Paradisal Peace. The opening of the *tahiyyah* announces the reintegration of all the good that God had manifested of Himself for the sake of our representing Him on earth. In other words, as in the last movement of the *hadrah*, body and soul have been reabsorbed into the Spirit on their way of return to our own Transpersonal Essence.

Clearly the first thing to be done on entering among the slaves of God is to address the Prophet, and the *tahiyyah* allows us to speak to him more directly than at any other time. In this world the normal greeting, *Peace be upon you* is a prayer, the plural 'you' being necessary to include not only the person in question but also the two guardian Angels, whereas the level of the *tahiyyah* altogether transcends the possibility of any evil that might need guarding against. We are therefore able to say, *Peace is upon thee, O Prophet, and the Mercy of God and His Blessings* and to affirm the same blessed truth with regard to ourselves and the other Saints who are now our companions.

The unsurpassably powerful testifications strengthened by the forefinger relate to the higher of the two Paradises, to the already quoted words *Enter thou My Paradise.* As to the second testification, it also concerns us inasmuch as a messenger by definition returns to his sender, and in this case the law of the *Sunnah* obliges us to follow him.

From these last words, as well as from the closing paragraphs taken as a whole, it becomes clear why the *salah* is referred to by the Prophet as the *mi'raj al-mu'min,* 'the Celestial Ascent of the believer.'

LITERARY CONTRIBUTIONS OF MARTIN LINGS

The Book of Certainty: The Sufi Doctrine of Faith, Vision and Gnosis (Written originally in Arabic. First English translation published, 1952.)

A Sufi Saint of the Twentieth Century: Shaikh Ahmad al-Alawi (1961)

Ancient Beliefs and Modern Superstitions (1964)

Shakespeare in the Light of Sacred Art (1966)

The Elements and Other Poems (1967)

The Heralds and Other Poems (1970)

Islamic Calligraphy and Illumination (1971)

What is Sufism? (1975)

The Qur'anic Art of Calligraphy and Illumination (1976)

Muhammad: His Life Based on the Earliest Sources (1983)

The Secret of Shakespeare (1984)

Collected Poems (1987)

The Eleventh Hour: The Spiritual Crisis of the Modern World in the Light of Tradition and Prophecy (1989)

Symbol and Archetype: A Study of the Meaning of Existence (1991)

The Sacred Art of Shakespeare: To Take Upon Us the Mystery of Things (1998)

Collected Poems: Revised and Augmented (2002)

Mecca: From before Genesis until Now (2004)

Sufi Poems: A Medieval Anthology (Compiled and Translated by Martin Lings, 2004)

Splendours of Qur'an Calligraphy and Illumination (2004)

A Return to the Spirit: Questions and Answers (2005)

Forthcoming

Symbol and Archetype: A Study of the Meaning of Existence (New, expanded edition, 2006)

The Sacred Art of Shakespeare: To Take Upon Us the Mystery of All Things (New, expanded edition, 2006)

The Underlying Religion (2006)

The Essential Martin Lings (2007)

Martin Lings in his home in Cairo, Egypt.

The view from the garden at the Giza home.

The Lings home in Giza, Cairo, Egypt.

Martin Lings as boy in England.

The garden at the Lings home in Kent, England.